BATH

MIDFORD

WELLOW
SHOSCOMBE HALT
RADSTOCK
MIDSOMER NORTON
CHILCOMPTON
EGAR
BURY

TROWBRIDGE

W I L T S

WESTBURY

WARMINSTER

HEYTESBURY
CODFORD

Salisbury
Plain

Stonehenge

BULFORD
(Military Sc)

AMESBURY

TIDWORTH

BULFORD
(Military Sc)

NEWTON
TONY

HEPTON MALLET

Frome

Witham

R. AVON

EVERCREECH

EVERCREECH JUNCTION

COLE

ZEALS

MERE

Hindon

DINTON

WILTON

SALISBURY

R. Nadder

MILFORD
(GOODS)

PORT

SEMLEY

TISBURY

DOWNT

WINCANTON

GILLINGHAM

SHAFTESBURY

REAMORE
B

INGBRIDGE

OMBE

HENSTRIDGE

STALBRIDGE

W I L T

FORD

DAGGON

ROAD

New
LYNDH
Forest
PN MALT

L

SHERBORNE

eybank

STURMINSTER
NEWTON

SHILLINGSTONE

Cranborne

STOURPAINE HALT

E

VERWOOD

ASHLEY HEATHWOOD
BROCKE

ne Abbas

BLANDFORD

S

WEST MOORS

LMSLEY
SW

den
nton

CHARLTON MARSHALL HALT

SPETTISBURY

BAILEY GATE
CORFE MULLEN HALT

BROADSTONE

WIMBORNE

R. Stour

POKESDOWN

HUR

NEW
MILTON

HINTON

R. Trent

HAMWORTHY JUNC

HOLTON HEATH

B'MOUTH
CENT

CHRISTCHURCH

R. Frome

TER

MORETON

WOOL

WAREHAM

Poole
Harbour

PARKSTONE

BANKS

BOURNEMOUTH
WEST

den

UPWEY JUNCTION

CORFE
CASTLE

Studland
Bay

ts-gr

21/23

Reminiscences of the Somerset & Dorset

Alan Hammond

Millstream Books

First Published 1997
by
Millstream Books
18 The Tyning
Bath BA2 6AL

© Alan Hammond 1997

Set in Palatino and printed by The Matthews Wright Press, Chard, Somerset

ISBN 0 948975 45 8

British Library Cataloguing-in-Publication Data:
A catalogue record for this book is available from the British Library

The gardens at Evercreech Junction were quite a feature. Vic Freak (left) and Ern Phillips tend the flower beds, overseen by stationmaster Jack Pike. In the background with the barrow is Colin Brine. (V.Freak collection)

(previous page): 2P, No 40634, and BR Standard class 5, No 73051, head the southbound Pines Express across Tucking Mill Viaduct on 3rd September 1955. (R.E.Toop)

INTRODUCTION & ACKNOWLEDGEMENTS

After my previous Somerset & Dorset books, *S&D Memories* and *Stories of the Somerset & Dorset*, I thought I would put my pen away. But I have had so many calls and letters from people who would like to see another volume, so here it is. It has really been a privilege to meet so many people who enjoyed their working life on the S&D. The friendliness I encountered while compiling all three of these books has been given in true S&D fashion.

While interviewing many of the contributors, the bad winter of 1962/3 always came into the conversation, so in this volume I have given special emphasis to events surrounding that period. But there are also plenty of other stories from many different grades of railwaymen and women covering various aspects of their time on the S&D through five decades.

However, before we meander down this most famous and beautiful cross-country railway, I would like to thank the many people who have helped me. First and foremost are all the contributors who made this book possible; it has been a pleasure and an experience to listen to all your wonderful stories. I would like to thank all the photographers who have allowed me to use their superb photographs, with a special thank-you to David Walden, David Milton, Ron Toop and John Stamp, as well as Laurie Poulton of the S&D Trust, East Anglia Group, for access to the Rimmer Collection. I am very grateful to Len Barry for producing so many prints for me. Thanks also to my publisher, Tim Graham, who has again supported, encouraged and advised me in the writing of this book; to Andy Moon, whose knowledge of the S&D has helped me in checking the manuscript and who also assisted with captions for the photographs; and to Alan Summers who has given me much helpful advice.

My thanks, too, to Roy Pitman of the S&D Trust who again found many more names and addresses of S&D railwaymen and women up and down the country. The Trust, based at Washford on the delightful West Somerset line, is where for me it all began. It has been a major factor in keeping the memory of the S&D alive. And a big thank-you to former S&D staff, Maurice Cook, Fred and Joan Fisher, Vic Freak, Paul Fry, Ron Gray, Gordon Hatcher, Fred Lester, Emily Poole, Eddie Skinner, Cliff Smith, Betty Spiller and Frank Staddon, all of whom had to answer many phone calls and letters from me asking for more information.

Since I started this journey of S&D memories some eight years ago, I have become good friends with many of the people mentioned in my books, but unfortunately when one passes away it becomes more personal. Donald Beale, Arthur Bowen, Vic Burt, Archie and Tom Gunning, Walt Jeans, Ted Lambert, Sam Lane, Ken Norris, Steve Penny, Harold (Nobby) Whiting and my great friend Will Locke were giants of their era who made the Somerset & Dorset railway the folklore it is today, and with this in mind this book is dedicated to all who worked on the S&D.

Last but not least, thanks to my wife Christine who has had to live with my obsession with the S&D and again without whose word-processing skills this book would still be in illegible handwriting. She has been a marvellous help to me and has supported me greatly in this new book of memories. I hope you enjoy them.

Alan Hammond, February 1997

This book follows the memories of 32 Somerset & Dorset railwaymen and women in chronological sequence of their first employment on the railway, from 1925 to 1962. A full index of their names and of all others mentioned in the book appears on pages 94 to 96.

Jinty, No 47557, stands after being retrieved from a giant snowdrift north of Winsor Hill in the winter of 1963. Chargeman fitter Howard Hiscox stands deep in the snow looking very cold. (J.Stamp)

1925

Fred Preater – Wagon Examiner

I joined the S&D as an oiler and grease boy in the carriage and wagon department at Bath Green Park on 15th November 1925; I was 14 years of age. Fortunately I lived in Brook Road which was only a few minutes walk to work. We worked in groups of two and my mate was Wilf Lee who lived a couple of doors away from me.

When passenger trains came into Bath Green Park station, Wilf and myself would fill all the axle boxes with oil; these were located on each step board on the various carriages. There was a hinge on these boards which we used to pull up so we could put our hand into a dark hole to fill the axle boxes up. Once a month carriages had to be serviced. We would draw out the oil pads making sure we put a tray on the step board so no oil would go onto it. These oil pads were located in the oil boxes on the frame underneath the coaches. We examined the pads making sure that they were in good condition and if not we would go to the grease house where spare pads would be taken from a tank of oil, not a very clean job. We would also polish all vacuum pistons with hemp rope. The examiner would go along the side of each carriage and tap all the wheels and examine the underframe. In those days we made sure that passenger safety came first. It was one of those jobs that people hardly ever saw, but it was an important part of railway work. There were four examiners there at the time: Fred Turland, Jim Watkins, Joe White and Jim Mogg. The stationmaster there at the time was Mr Davis.

Grease containers were put in various places in Bath yard and it was our job as greasers to ensure that they were always full. There were 20 lbs of grease in each tin and woe betide you if any of the tins were empty. On Wednesdays and Saturdays, the messroom which was by the side of the river Avon had to be scrubbed out, the floor had to be spotless, the brass had to shine and the stove had to be black-leaded.

Whilst at Bath Green Park I joined the St John Ambulance brigade of which I was a member for 53 years. I recall two occasions where my knowledge of first aid was able to assist others; unfortunately one is a terrible memory. In November 1929 I was in Bath yard working with Fred Gibbons who was the relief station foreman and also our superintendent of the St John Ambulance. The goods inspector was John Norman who tragically lost his life in this accident. A class 7F engine, No 89, hauling a coal train, ran away after the driver and fireman were overcome by fumes in Combe Down tunnel. It came into Bath yard out of control. Christopher Wagner, the guard on this train, knew there was trouble as it was travelling much faster than usual when it was passing the Co-op siding. He jumped from his van and broke both legs but survived. The 7F hurtled into the goods yard at speed, overturned and crashed into the yard inspector's office. Fortunately Fred was not in his office. A few of us rushed over to the cab of the engine which was now lying on its side. After some time we got the driver Henry Jennings and fireman Maurice Pearce out. Their clothes were badly burnt and they were both in a bad way, hardly recognizable. We took them to the cabin where first aid was administered until the ambulance arrived. We then went out looking for the guard who was found and rushed to hospital. Sadly Henry Jennings died along with John Norman who was trying to save others in the yard, but was hit and killed instantly by the runaway engine. Another casualty was Jack Loader, a railway clerk who was crossing the goods yard at the time and was struck by debris from the runaway engine.

In 1931 I was made redundant and rejoined the S&D in June 1947. I was promoted to an examiner and transferred to Radstock. Part of my duties was to walk from Radstock to Writhlington, Braysdown and Midsomer Norton to examine all the coal wagons from the collieries around this area. One Saturday morning at Radstock a labourer was unloading sugar beet from a wagon and a fellow worker accidently put a pitch fork through his arm. His arm was in a bad way but I treated him immediately, stopping the heavy flow of blood. If I had not been there I doubt if he would have survived. I had a letter from the railway thanking me for my prompt action.

I enjoyed my work at Radstock. Some of the men there that I recall were Charlie Rawlings, Charlie Baker, Aubrey Pearce, Jack Kemp and Bill Beeho. In February 1952 I moved back to Bath Green Park and stayed there until closure in 1966. I am now 85 years of age; my S&D memories have always stayed with me, it was a happy time in my life.

General view of Bath Green Park motive power depot with the running lines on the extreme left. 4F, No 44422, stands against loco coal wagons. Two breakdown coaches are parked next to the shed with a Jinty close by. An Ivatt tank has just left the station with a local train. All this is surveyed by a solitary figure standing by the signalpost on the right. (D.Walden)

1934

Bernard Ware – Guard

My father Henry John Ware joined the S&D at Henstridge in 1904 and retired in 1955 as deputy chief controller at Bath Green Park. My father came home from work one day and said there was a job as a junior porter at Wincanton station, so in July 1934 I joined; another porter there at the time was Dick Player.

The duties consisted of cleaning and assisting loadings in the goods shed. I was only at Wincanton one week, then moved to Evercreech Junction (Bill Cornell who was a friend of my father was the station foreman) where for the rest of the summer I carried out general station duties. Then I moved on to Warmley which was on the LMS line. I took the job over from my great friend Fred Davis. I was at Warmley for a short while, when I received a letter from Derby staff office telling me I had to take a position in the Birmingham area or a week's notice. That's how the LMS treated you then. The wages at the time were £1 1s a week. I accepted the position, but wasn't sent to Birmingham. Instead I was ordered to Bristol Temple Meads as a towel boy. When the LMS trains arrived it was our job as towel boys to remove all towels, clean or dirty, and soap from the carriages. Then before departure we had to place clean towels and soap in the toilets.

My next move was to Yate, still as a junior porter. Sometime early in 1937 I took up the position of porter signalman at Ashley Hill on the Avonmouth line. In spring 1938 I returned to the S&D as a signalman at Writhlington and Braysdown where I remained until January 1940. It was an easy position; the hours were 8.00am to 4.00pm and there was never any shortage of coal for the signalbox as the supplies came from Braysdown pit. I remember Sunday 3rd September 1939, the day war broke out. I was sent for to open up the signalbox. A special train loaded with timber was brought out and shunted into the sidings for safety reasons. The powers that be thought there would be an air raid and the train would be safer in Writhlington Sidings.

The stationmaster at Radstock was Mr H Lewis; other Radstock men I remember were drivers Charlie Rawlings, Norman Cook, David Jones who came from Blackpool, shunter Bert Ash and fireman Fred Beard.

One person that comes to mind at that time was Harry Clark, a member of the permanent way gang. One day after the war had started I went to the signalbox window, and shouted out to Harry, "they're coming". The sound of distant planes could be heard. Harry cocked his ear and said "no, sonny, they're our's. When them Germans come over you will hear the drone of their planes with diesel engines". How true that proved later on in the war, especially during the air raids when I was on duty at Bristol Barrow Lane Sidings signalbox in 1940.

Whilst at Writhlington signalbox, I recall a young signalman at Radstock East called Steve Jones who hailed from Walsall. One day stationmaster Mr Lewis asked him what he would do if there was an air raid on. Steve, always full of fun and jokes, replied "I shall run down those 30 steps sharply and into the toilet, and put the engaged sign on the door". Steve was a lovely lad, we were mates when I was at Hazelwell signalbox in 1942. I believe he died at quite a young age, a great shame.

From Writhlington I had a few years at Hazelwell and Northfield and returned to Bath on the S&D in May 1946, as a second class relief signalman. I saw duty at Bath Junction, Midford, Wellow, Midsomer Norton, Chilcompton, Binegar and Shepton Mallet (Waterloo Road) signalboxes.

BR Standard class 4, No 75072, stands at Midford in the summer of 1965. The driver converses with the signalman while the guard in the background seems impatient to be off. (D.Walden)

I had a short time back at Northfield then returned to Midford signalbox in January 1947 to meet up with colleagues Percy Savage and Harry Wiltshire. That year we experienced a real bad winter; the snow plough just kept going to and fro over the worst spots. On my arrival at Midford the main signalboxes over the S&D were open continuously for eight weeks which included Sundays. By this arrangement the S&D over the Mendips never got snowed under.

I remember, one week, the order to stay open over the weekend came as late as Saturday afternoon, which meant that arriving home that evening, I had to prepare to return on Sunday at 6.00am. When I got up for duty, I found fresh snow had fallen to a depth of about nine inches. I had a very slow ride on my motorbike and when turning into the lane leading to Midford box, I swung around and came off in about one foot of snow. Dear old Percy Savage was standing there enjoying a good laugh.

Another time on early turn I found the snow too deep to ride so I walked to Bath Junction hoping to catch the 5.50am freight. Bill Wilds greeted me saying "the 3.30am is about to leave, it's only a single load". I went over to the driver who to my surprise was a good mate, Dennis Clem; he welcomed me on board and off we went. On arrival at Midford I alighted and Harry Wiltshire took my place on the footplate where he got a lift home to Wellow. To complete the day I had a lift home on the snow plough engine returning to Bath with driver Osmond Pitt who told me at one point the snow was so deep that they had come to a standstill.

The coldest night during this period was a Sunday. I had the coal fire stove flat out, an oil heater and three oil lamps, (there was no electricity in those days). Although Midford signalbox was not very large, with all the heat on, we still had frost on some of the windows. When I went out to start my motorbike and gave it the first kick start, it didn't spring back – it was frozen. I eventually got it going and when I got home both my coat and myself were frozen stiff.

I remained at Midford signalbox until spring 1948, then I moved back to Bath Junction signalbox until January 1957. I believe I am correct in stating that this was a very busy period with more people taking holidays. Summer Saturdays were hectic and freight traffic heavy which meant weekend working.

In 1957 I left signalbox work for health reasons. After some time off work I returned as a porter at Bitton station. My next move was back to good old Bath Green Park as a parcels porter. There was plenty to do with large amounts of parcel traffic from Stothert and Pitt, the crane people. There was also lots of luggage from the various colleges at the end of each term and we also transported racing pigeons in season. This was all extra parcel traffic and whenever the station foreman was off sick or on leave it was the parcel porter who relieved him. It was a job that I liked doing, especially working with stationmasters Paul Pearman and George Robertson.

I was appointed passenger guard at Bath in 1960, but did not take up the position until 1962. In fact I was road learning and enjoying the ride on the last up Pines Express when Peter Smith was driving. I passed for guard duties in November 1962 and my first turn as a passenger guard was on a BR class 5MT 4–6–0, No 73051, with driver Den Norris of Templecombe.

The week commencing Monday 24th December 1962 was the start of the very bad winter with snow starting to fall heavily. I was with driver Arthur

Jinty No 47276, coupled to an unidentified Stanier 8F, takes water at Shepton Mallet during the winter of 1963. Fireman Ian Bunnett has the unenviable task of placing the hose in the tank. (J.Stamp)

2P, No 40568, and West Country Combe Martin, *No 34043, haul a Bournemouth train away from Midford on 26th June 1954. Standing at the signal is light engine 4F No 44166. (R.E.Toop)*

Selman in charge of SR Bulleid Pacific *Combe Martin*, No 34043, on the 6.48am. On Friday 28th December I was with driver Len England with a strange engine, a Maunsell class 'Q' 0–6–0, No 30541. We left Bath at 7.05am, 17 minutes late, and arrived at Templecombe at 9.21, 40 minutes late. Mind you the snow was bad over the Mendips. On Saturday night, 29th, and Sunday 30th came the great blizzards. When I reported for duty on Monday 31st everything was in a muddle.

The blockage by snow over the Mendips was a trying time. In the week commencing 7th January 1963 we began running our usual turns, though there was quite a lot of late running. On 19th January, I worked the 4.37pm Bath to Templecombe passenger train with driver David Hadfield on a BR class 4MT 4–6–0 engine, No 75071. We arrived at Templecombe at 6.45, 26 minutes late, mainly still due to the bad snow conditions over the Mendips. There was no 8.25pm Templecombe to Derby 'Perishables' booked to run on Saturdays. It was a regular turn for the engine to run light from Templecombe to Bath. Driver John Stamp and fireman Trevor Davies on a BR class 5MT 4–6–0, No 73052, were waiting for me and we departed from Templecombe at 6.50. We plodded along and every so often John would come over and look at the down line and remark, "it's filling in". In places nothing could be seen of the down line metals, they were completely covered with snow.

It wasn't actually snowing much, but when the winds got up it blew the snow from the fields onto the line. However just past Ham Wood Viaduct I never experienced anything like it, our class 5 must have hit a deep drift as she appeared to rise up like a horse. We didn't come off the track, but just kept plodding on. The three of us on the cab laughed our heads off; we found we were standing in nearly a foot of snow which had been forced onto the footplate. We arrived back at Bath Green Park safely at about 8.00pm, glad to get home.

Well things went on, but one could see the poor old S&D was being killed off, with signalboxes closed and less and less freight, although local passenger traffic kept up fairly well. Then the notices of closure arrived and everyone got ready for the last day of normal service on 1st January 1966.

At the last moment one of the bus companies that was to take over once the train service ended, had pulled out. Instead of Western Region management keeping the same service on they applied an emergency service, which I believe was about four up and four down, stopping passenger trains per day. We at Bath had about three duties with six passenger guards; they were Roy Woolley, Charlie Davis, Jack Hopkins, Bert Veasey, Fred Rooke and myself. We more or less took it in turns to work until notices were published. Then it finally came through that scheduled services would finish on 5th March 1966.

However several specials were arranged for Sunday 6th March 1966. I was rostered to work the 10.30am Bath to Bournemouth and 3.20pm Bournemouth to Bath, with drivers Bill Gunning and Archie Gunning who were on ex-LMS 8F 2–8–0 engine, No 48706, and BR Standard class 4MT 2–6–4T, No 80043.

BR Standard class 4 tank, No 80043, provides the backdrop for drivers Bill and Archie Gunning on the occasion of the SLS excursion on the final weekend of the S&D, 6th March 1966. (M.Beale)

I only wish I had had a camera with me. I can remember going past my old signalbox of Writhlington and Braysdown. We stopped at Shepton Mallet for a photo call and I made a short recorded speech for the BBC. We finally arrived at Bournemouth Central. I remember meeting Alf Metcalf there who was a retired Bournemouth passenger guard. I had first met Alf when I was a towel boy at Bristol Temple Meads and he was an LMS parcel porter.

This time I really don't think we believed our dear S&D was to be no more. Departure from Bournemouth was at 4.20pm, one hour late. I was too sad to remember much about the journey except for Sturminster Newton, a station right to the last. It was well used by passengers. I shall never forget looking out and seeing all these people end to end on the station with the local policeman and the village parson standing there as if he was with his flock, a moment I shall cherish forever. We arrived at Bath Green Park at 6.50, some 66 minutes late. I remember creeping away, with just a short wave to brothers Bill and Archie Gunning. There was nobody to greet us, no local press or television; management had won, the S&D had just died.

On Monday 7th March 1966 we all reported for duty. With nothing to do, we drank a lot of tea. The station was deadly quiet with no engines or coaches. At 3.00pm someone from Bath Spa came over and presented me with a letter which said I'd been allocated a passenger guard position at Bristol Temple Meads. I was to report at 9.00am on Tuesday 8th March 1966.

I remember the next day going to the station and picking up my kit, and all quiet, lonely and very sad, off I went. I finished the rest of my working life at Bristol, ending as a conductor guard in July 1982. I had spent 48 years on the railway.

I often walk through Bath Green Park station, which is now a car park and market. As I walk down the old platform my thoughts go back to the old S&D steam days.

1934

Maurice Cook – Driver

The 'Perishable' was a train that we worked from Highbridge to Templecombe in the 1940s. It was quite interesting because things were different each day. The engine for this job was one that had worked from Templecombe in the morning and could be one of five various engines, such as an old Southern Region 1PT, Ivatt 2PT, 4–4–0P, 3F or 4F. Our first stop was at Bason Bridge where we would carry out some shunting and then pick up about eight loaded milk tanks. Further along the line at Glastonbury more shunting and loading took place.

It was on this turn we started to put potatoes and onions on the firebox to bake. When we reached Templecombe the shunters liked the smell of our goodies, so we had to cook some for them.

I remember once going from the down to the up road to get to Highbridge shed with driver Lou Moxey. We had to go about 50 yards beyond the points to clear the track circuit. We could see the signalman Harry Brown trying to work the points, but he was unable to move them. I then remembered that earlier that day a weedkilling train had been over the branch. I got down from the cab and wiped the four ends of the rails which cleared the track circuit. The signalman was then able to pull the points and give us a green flag to set back to the loco box. The lineman Tom Strike had been sent for and when he arrived I explained to him what I had done. He said: "Thanks, you saved me a walk." I think the weedkiller had a wetting agent added to it that had broken the track circuit, the same sort of thing that happens today when wet leaves get crushed at the end of the track circuits.

On Sundays at Highbridge we had two milk turns; on the morning one we went over to the GWR to pick up empty milk tanks. The first thing that the shunters had to do when we were attached was to pull the strings to reduce the vacuum in the brake cylinders as the GWR worked on 25 inches and the LMS and others on 21 inches. We then took them to Bason Bridge milk siding where they were cleaned and filled, and we returned to Highbridge. On the afternoon turn we had to go to Bason Bridge to pick up the loaded tanks which we normally took on to Templecombe to transfer to the Southern Region.

On 16th May 1965 I was on this afternoon turn. We had an Ivatt class 2MT, No 41296; my fireman was Bill Conibeer. We picked up the loaded milk tanks at Bason Bridge and on this occasion we had to take them to Highbridge to transfer to the GWR. On this particular day the Great Western were altering their layout and because of this we had to wait nearly two hours before we could transfer the tanks. Once we had placed them in their siding, we made our way back to the S&D line. We had to pass over a catchpoint which protected the up main line. This had been uncoupled for permanent way work and an inspector had clipped and locked the point, but when we slowly moved over it, one of our pony wheels came off. The reason this happened was that the new rail was higher than the old one. As it was a Sunday it was difficult to get help, but after a long wait we were relieved. The next day we came on duty everything was back to normal.

Ivatt tank, No 41296, stands with its pony wheel derailed on the revised layout at Highbridge on 16th May 1965. Driver Maurice Cook surveys the scene with hands on hips. (R.Hawkins)

1935

Frank Staddon – Guard

It is nice to reflect on one's working life. At the age of 82 I look back on my 33 years spent on the Somerset & Dorset working as a porter and a guard; every day was different. My first encounter with railways was when I was a young boy at Binegar in 1919. There was a small railway connecting Oakhill Brewery. The 2ft 6in track was two miles long and it came from the brewery passing the *Mendip Inn* through Binegar bottom into Binegar goods shed for onward delivery. This railway closed in 1921. One of the drivers of these small engines (one named *Mendip*) was a family friend called Percy Purnell. The well-known bottles of stout were put on six wagons with a brakeman on the back for the journey to Binegar.

The brewery gave the railway staff a flagon of beer each day. One of the brakemen being very partial to his drink would finish his allowance and then drink everybody else's. Percy and his friends, getting rather fed up about this, decided to get their own back on him (he was on braking duties with Percy). They filled up one of the flagons with a concoction of something revolting which he drank before they left. Halfway across the Mendips on their way to Binegar, Percy heard this shouting and moaning coming from the brakeman to stop the train. Of course Percy didn't hear this and took him all the way to the goods shed. When reaching Binegar the brakeman was seen running full pelt to the station toilet and their flagons of ale were never interfered with again.

I became a relief porter at Binegar in the 1930s. There were 17 staff there at the time. One of them, Charlie Rawles, was always complaining that he had trouble with his legs. Being keen and young and feeling sorry for Charlie I always offered to do the distant signal for him, which was about a mile away, to save his old legs. After one long trip from the distant signal, there was Charlie off home after his shift. He was like a two-year old going down the lane, he couldn't walk fast enough. I had to laugh. But Charlie would always help you out. One day I wanted to go to the May Fair at Wells with my girlfriend, now my wife (Doris and I have been married 57 years). I asked him if he would change shifts with me. "No problem" he said, a packet of five Woodbines changed hands and off I went to the May Fair.

Frank Staddon poses in Binegar Road, c.1935. To the right is the Horse and Jockey *pub where landlord Herbie Carter used to serve scrumpy. (F.Staddon collection)*

Other men who worked at Binegar in the 1930s were stationmaster Mr Christopher Oxford, junior clerk Ray Batt, clerk Roy Gould, signalmen Jim Garland, Charlie Attwood and Edgar Smith, permanent way men Bill Southway, Jack Foxhall and ganger Sam Tucker.

One of the stations I worked at as a relief porter was Bridgwater. In those days there was plenty of work. They had a carman who would come in with his little flat lorry. We used to handle wagon loads of grain and he would shout out: "Come on Frank, give us a hand." He was only a short chap but he could pick up a two-cwt sack of grain and have no trouble in putting it onto his lorry, whereas I would pick it up from the bay, have it put on my shoulder, stagger a few yards and collapse to the ground.

Johnson tank, No 58072, ready to leave Bridgwater with a rake of wagons in 1952. Note the shunting bell sign at the base of the signal. (H.C.Casserley)

I remember another time whilst working at Bridgwater there were lots of factories making wicker products. Having a look around one day I noticed a nice linen basket which cost 5/−. I bought the basket but the trouble was trying to get it home. I got a train to Wells then tied it onto the back of my Hercules bicycle and cycled the six miles to Binegar. There is a little story about this linen basket. When we moved to Bath in 1939 the basket was put in our bedroom. When the Bath blitz was on in April 1942 our terraced house got bombed and machine gunned. After coming out of the shelter we made our way to the house. Looking up the stairs there was a spray of bullets going into our bedroom. One of the bullets had penetrated the linen basket and made a hole in it, but it did not destroy it as we still use it today in 1997, 55 years on, so I have never forgotten my Bridgwater days.

I remember one job in 1946. I was sent out to Common Lane crossing, near Templecombe, for relief crossing duties. Malcolm Hatherall, porter at Evercreech Junction, was to carry out the day duties and I had the night turn.

When I arrived there from Bath to relieve Malcolm I asked him: "Where do I go". He replied: "The crossing keeper's house is locked up as they are on holiday; the only place left to sit down through the night to look after the crossing is the outside toilet," and that is where I stayed for my 12-hour shift. Fortunately the turn was only for a week.

Another memory of Malcolm always makes me smile. He and I were both working at Bath Weston station on the same day, but on different shifts. Part of the job was collecting tickets. I went into work the next day and Reg Ashford from control phoned up to ask if I was on late turn last night. I replied: "No, Reg, I was on early turn, Malcolm was on late turn. Why what's the problem?" He replied. "Well, there was a bit of a to-do on the platform last night. Colonel Mountstevens was coming in on the train. He is a big railway official and when he reached the gate Malcolm asked the gentleman for his ticket. The Colonel showed him a gold medallion on a chain but Malcolm said to the Colonel: "That's no good to me, I've got a football medal and you won't get by with one of them." The Colonel was lost for words and lost his temper. He said to Malcolm: "If you go into your office and look at your railway papers it will give you a list of all medallions authorizing certain personnel of British Railways to travel." Sure enough that was correct and poor old Malcolm never lived it down.

When I was working as a porter/guard on the old push-and-pull from Wells to Glastonbury in the 1940s a lady wanted a return ticket which in those days cost 3d. She gave me what I thought was a threepenny bit but when I balanced up at the end of the trip I had a good look at this coin; it was a silver fourpenny piece and this was the one and only time I ever saw one. I thought I wouldn't pay it in, so I put 3d in out of my own pocket to make the books good. Next day on the 10.30am the same lady got on the train and came up to me and said how upset she was. She was off to Glastonbury to retrace her movements so she could find what she had lost yesterday. I replied: "What was that?" and she said: "A fourpenny piece." I replied: "Don't worry, my dear." I took it out of my railway purse and returned it to her; she was over the moon. As a reward she gave me a shilling which I declined but she insisted I have it.

Whilst at Wells I joined the S&D ambulance team under a very nice chap called Bob Fry who was a guard at Wells. He was a very keen and capable ambulance man. Other members of the team were driver Harry Pearce and porter Harry Curtis. On one occasion we reached the divisional finals held at Shepton Mallet. We had to administer first aid to two people who were both injured in falls. We did very well and came runners-up to the Radstock team of Charlie Rawlings, Fred Beard, Wally Moon and Fred Griffin. The best individual of the final was our captain Bob Fry. For coming second we were presented with a nice tray of fish knives and forks. Another team there were the Highbridge lads, made up of Frank Jones, Bill May, Chummy Andrews and Jock Kirkbright. The first aid knowledge I learnt at Wells stood me in good stead for the rest of my railway career.

I became a guard in the war years and I worked many ambulance trains across the S&D and also trains full of prisoners of war. I recall one day when we took a train full of prisoners to Blandford Forum where they had an army camp. We had 12 bogies on with 600 German soldiers. When we reached Blandford they all disembarked onto the platform. I shall never forget one British sergeant-major shouting out to a bunch of these prisoners: "Form in fours, get in order." When one prisoner fell to the floor, after slipping, the sergeant-major went up to him and said: "Get up you lazy sod, you haven't come here to sleep, get in line and march."

We used to work American troop trains from Bath to Bournemouth. We enjoyed working these trains. The first-class carriages were filled with American girls equivalent to our ATS girls and as soon as they left the train we made our way to their carriages. These girls were supplied with big slabs of chocolate and often they would leave them on the tables when they didn't want them. I had a little girl of 12 months and chocolate was unheard of so it was nice to take some home for her. Also these girls only used packets of 20 cigarettes and would toss packets of five away, so it was a little bonus working these wartime trains.

One occurrence that I will never forget happened in the 1950s. I was a goods guard at the time. The driver that day was my old mate Reg Beasley and we were working coal trains back and forth from Bath to Midsomer Norton, stopping at Radstock where we picked up some coal wagons to take on to Bath, normally four journeys in a shift. On one of the stops at Radstock we were just about to leave when Radstock railwayman Bill Beeho came over to me. Bill lived at Shoscombe Single Hill halt with his wife Margaret whose job it was to look after the halt. Bill asked me whether I could take a couple of disused wagon timbers and drop them off at the halt. "I can't manage them on my bike," he said, with a twinkle in his eye. "It would be a shame to leave

7F, No 53807, passes Midsomer Norton heading south with a short freight train. (R.E.Toop)

them here rotting when they'd make a lovely bit of firewood." I replied: "Of course, Bill," so we manoeuvred the two wooden timbers, which were each about four feet long, into the guards van. I gave the green flag to Reg, a thumbs up to Bill and we set sail for Bath with our 50 coal wagons. Coming up to Shoscombe and Single Hill halt the class 7F with Reg up front was going at a fair speed. Into the halt I got these two wooden wagon timbers and pushed them off onto the platform (I thought), but once they touched the platform they took off with speed. I looked on with utter horror as they launched themselves off the platform into the nearby road. Thank goodness there was no road traffic at that moment or there could have been a nasty accident. I never ever threw anything off the guards van again. I still have visions even in 1997 of those two wagon timbers flying through the air; what a fright!

I remember a derailment at Midsomer Norton. We were going through there with engine and van. Harry Shearn was my driver and on reaching the station we were held up whilst Percy Hamblin the Midsomer Norton signalman let a light engine which was being used for banking duties cross the road before the Pines Express was due, which should not have been a problem. Unfortunately whilst crossing the road the light engine had split the points and got derailed; there was panic stations all around. I got off my van and ran up to the incident to see what had happened. The stationmaster, who was a relief Western man, said: "We will have to get the Pines down on the wrong road." I replied: "Excuse me for interfering, sir, but you won't get the Pines past there; you haven't got the clearance." He then went into a state of panic. "What am I going to do?" he asked. I replied: "Would you like me to try and pull it clear for you?" He replied: "You won't reach it with a screw coupling" but I said: "Don't worry about that, tell Percy to let us come in so we can take the engine and van up to the derailment." Whilst Harry took the engine through I went into the coal yard and disconnected a link coupling from a coal wagon. Harry went up as far as he could to the light engine. I then put the link coupling through the screw coupling and just managed to get it over the hook of the banking engine. I then said to Harry: "Take her back steady, she will come" and she did, clearing space on the down road for the Pines Express. The stationmaster patted me on the back and said: "Thank goodness you were here today, Frank. I wouldn't have known what to do." The Pines was then brought up from Chilcompton and was soon on its way to Bath and Manchester. I learnt this trick from another S&D man, Bob Green. It was fortunate I did this as the derailment happened on a busy summer Saturday and if instant action had not been carried out the whole line would have been at a standstill for many hours.

Another trip I recall in the 1950s was when working the 9.00pm up train from Bournemouth West to Bath. I was enjoying a cup of tea in the porter's cabin on Bournemouth West station when I heard this almighty bang. I thought it was a bomb going off; it made me fall to the ground. I picked myself up and rushed outside. I have never seen anything like it. At the bottom end of the platform two coaches had come off the rails, one had gone out into the roadway and the other one had gone over the blocks blocking the platform. Another six coaches behind them were luckily still on the rails. Apparently what had happened was that these coaches and brake van had been shunted down from

Bournemouth West in summer 1964. Two rebuilt West Country Pacifics, one of them No 34047 Callington, stand in the station before working trains to Waterloo. To the left stands Bulleid coach set 822. (D.Walden)

Branksome and somebody, for whatever reason, hadn't coupled up the coaches to the shunting engine. As the engine pushed away, the eight coaches went speeding away under their own steam. Nearing the station the porter/guard in the brake van who was controlling the brake looked out of the window. On seeing no engine behind him he immediately put the brake on hard, and then had the presence of mind to lay flat on the floor of the brake van, away from the three-foot iron stand that was in the middle of the van where the brake was situated. Fortunately for him this probably saved his life, because that structure was crushed on impact. After getting out of the van he dived into the parcels office and just collapsed with shock. Happily, neither he nor anybody else was hurt, a lucky escape for everybody. I never heard the outcome of the incident.

We had a nice old guard at Bath called Ted Parsons. On one occasion in the 1950s Ted was working the 7.00pm passenger train from Bath to Templecombe in the week before Christmas. When he arrived at Evercreech New, a lady got off the train with her Christmas shopping and her young son. In Bath she had bought him a torch with a changeable red, green and white light. When the lad got onto the platform he switched the green light on and started waving the torch about. The next thing that happened was the driver touching the whistle and off the train went towards Evercreech Junction leaving poor old Ted Parsons on the platform flabbergasted. The driver thought Ted was waving a green light to go. Poor old Ted had his leg pulled many times in the various cabins up and down the S&D.

Another personality was guard Larry Maggs. Now some mornings Larry was in his guards van going up the line and I would pass him on the down line in my guards van. At a certain point on the line both trains would slow down or sometimes come to a standstill and we would often shout out to each other and have a jaw. Now it was near Derby day, and Larry's train was at a standstill. Looking out of my van there was Larry, his railway cap on back to front, legs astride on the buffer of his van shouting out: "Artic Prince to win the Derby, Artic Prince to win the Derby [1951]." I had a little flutter and Artic Prince came in first.

Percy (the Colonel) Savage was the well-liked signalman at Midford. I recall a story he told me of when he got the fright of his life. It was in the 1950s. Percy was on nights in his box at Midford. It was a cold foggy winter's evening and Percy had just let the 10.30pm freight out. As there was nothing due until 3.00am, when the mail train came through, Percy decided to make himself comfortable on the locker. About 1.00am Percy heard this thump, thump, thump, then he heard some rattling going on outside the signalbox. He thought to himself, "what's happening?", and looked out of his window but could see nothing because of the thick fog. More thumping and now rattling of chains, then he heard somebody coming up the signalbox stairs. Suddenly there was a face with a long beard and white hair pressed hard against the window. Percy thought Old Nick was coming to get him. The door opened and this old boy said to Percy: "Excuse me, signalman, have you seen my goats, I've lost them." As Percy said to me, that's what the rattling was; the goats were running around attached to the chains. The goats were found and Percy made himself a strong cup of tea to steady his nerves.

On the last day of the S&D I was with my good mate driver Reg Beasley. We went to Wincanton and cleared out the sidings. We picked up about 23 wagons and worked them back to Bath. I was practically the last guard to bring a train into Bath Green Park, and I went into the office and shook hands with inspector Bill Wiltshire for the last time. It was a very sad day for both of us. We looked at each other and a few tears were shed, this was the end of a lifetime spent on a special railway for Bill and myself.

1935

Vic Burt – Driver

The four years I spent on the S&D were the happiest time out of my 40 years service on the railway which started in 1935.

I was a driver on the S&D in the shunting link at the sub depot at Templecombe Upper. Other colleagues there at the time were Maurice Miles, Gordon Hatcher, Robin Gould, Bill Goddard and Steve Penny. I also had two brothers Reg and Percy who both worked on the S&D. In the 1950s I went into a link of 12 turns; my fireman was Norman Light.

I remember one journey when we signed on to relieve Bath men at the lower platform at Templecombe. We were taking the mail train on to Bournemouth West. This train consisted of a mail and parcel van and loose-coupled freight. This particular morning we had a Southern West Country engine which was in a bad way, the safety valves were blowing and waking up the village of Templecombe. The engine was totally covered in steam. I told the Bath fireman one of his injectors wasn't working but he took no notice so I put it right. Looking at the boiler sight glass it appeared empty. Using the drain cock I could not bring down the water level, and using the top cock would not bring up the water level, so I put on the second injector. By the time we had ¾ level in the glass we had knocked the boiler pressure from 240 down to 160psi. How they never dropped the lead plugs, especially coming down to Templecombe on a falling gradient of about 1:50, I will never know. When we arrived at Bournemouth West it was the practice of the shunter to secure the train. After putting down several brakes on the wagons he would uncouple the engine and stand it off in the traders' siding. He would then allow the train to trickle by into one of the dead end sidings with the guard's help. This particular day we came unstuck; our goods train was the first train of the day, the rails were heavy with the morning dew, and the engine had no sand in the sand boxes (the Bath men had emptied these coming down). We applied the brakes but unfortunately the wheels picked up and we slid into the traders' siding slowly but heavily. We pushed the stop blocks back 20 feet and buffer-locked several wagons. It was not our day.

At Templecombe on 7th July 1959, BR Standard class 4, No 75072, with the 3.40pm train from Bournemouth passes a Maunsell brake third before reversing back into the station. (R.C.Riley)

The feeling amongst all the men on the S&D from Bath to Branksome, and on the branches to Bridgwater, Wells, and Highbridge, seemed to be the same – nothing was ever too much trouble for anyone and everybody went out of their way to be of help in any way they could. For example, I was living at Yeovil at the time and to be able to have a long weekend in the 12-week roster turns we had to sign on twice on the Monday at 3.00am and 10.00pm, the latter being for disposal and preparation of engines. Now the train for me to get back to Yeovil ran considerably after my turn had finished, but there was a train which left an hour before I booked off. Someone always came along and said: "Get going, I will hang on and finish your roster." Except for one morning in four years I was at home and in bed before my duty at Templecombe was finished, that's the kind of workmates they were.

When my time came to leave the S&D I had to return to Yeovil, but there were times when we took our engine down to Templecombe which enabled me to keep in touch with my old friends.

Unfortunately my next contact with the S&D was to help in the final rites. Having the knowledge of the layout I had to take down five bogie bolsters from Yeovil Junction to the site of work and bring the wagons back which had been loaded by the contractors the previous day. We off-loaded the rails and stacked them into the sidings and then used the wagons again the next day. The safety regulations laid down were that the contractors would not enter the section until we arrived with the wagons. One morning we entered a cutting with a Warship diesel but nobody informed us the contractors were working and, unable to stop in time, we hit their engine at about 20mph. The loaded track section was hanging out over the end of the wagons; all of them had to be re-stacked and there was a lot of damage to both diesels. Almost two years after, the contractors were still fighting to get compensation for their engine.

After the closure of Yeovil depot I moved to Westbury but it wasn't the same, especially seeing the Pines Express going via Basingstoke. I took early retirement in 1975 and went to work at Plessey Marine in the works police at Templecombe. Plessey had bought two units, one of them being the S&D depot. The engine shed had been rebuilt in 1950 in red brick and Plessey utilised this as the heavy machinery shop, boxing in one end of the building and installing a light roller door at the other end.

On nights when on patrol duty it was easy to imagine that you could hear the Poole goods clanking by or The Pines Express with its happy holiday-makers making for the sea at Bournemouth or the men on the footplate with the 2.40am mail train from Bath heading towards the Dorset countryside in the pitch black with only the glare of the firebox and the lights of passing farms and cottages. The noise of the depot alive with the steam and the laughter, what a happy time it was, all gone and never to return.

1935

Fred Epps – Driver

I had one bad experience that I have never forgotten, it nearly cost me my life. My driver Charlie Knight and myself were working the 10.30pm Bath to Templecombe goods train one Saturday evening in late 1944. We had a full load of 45 mixed freight wagons on with a banking engine driven by Edgar Gray attached to the rear. Our engine was a Fowler 7F 2–8–0, No 13808. It was an extremely long load that winter's evening; the train went from Bath yard gas works right past the station signalbox, a distance of about 200 yards. We were ready to go, the ground signal came off and Charlie blew the whistle to let the banking engine know we were on our way. Charlie moved the regulator and we started moving but we only went a short distance when the engine started to lurch about all over the place. (Charlie jumped off the engine which I didn't know at the time). I was thrown to the right and ended up hanging down over the side of the cab holding onto the hand rail. The engine was now

Fred Epps poses in front of No 75072 at Bath Green Park Motive Power Depot. (F.Epps collection)

pointing towards Bath gas works which was in the opposite direction. Suddenly everything stopped and there was an eerie silence with just the hissing of steam. When I looked around Charlie had gone, the engine was hanging over, being only supported by its trailing wheels against the check rails with the right hand buffer buried in the ground. The check rails were keeping the engine from falling right over, the tender was at an angle but fortunately the wagons were still on the rail. Anybody with any knowledge of steam engines would know that if the engine had turned right over I might have been crushed by 68 tons of locomotive. Thank goodness for that check rail. A crew of Bristol men who were waiting to leave on a 4F freight train across the track rendered assistance and got me out. Fortunately Charlie and I were unharmed. It was about 10.00am on the Sunday morning before they righted the engine. They had to get a big crane down from Derby to help put her back up. It was a bit of a mystery why this actually happened. On investigation they found a steel plate, three feet square and about half an inch thick, laying across the rails. The pony wheels had run over the plate and the wheels swung round towards the gasworks. They never found out where the plate had come from though they tried to trace any scrap wagons which may have passed over the line that day, but none had. Unofficially sabotage was suspected, but nothing was ever proved.

Standard class 4, possibly No 76011, draws into Stalbridge station on a murky June day in 1965 with a Bulleid three-coach set, heading north. (D.Walden)

Working on the footplate in World War Two meant long hours. I remember taking out an American troop train from Bath Green Park at 3.00am. The troops had to disembark at several places, one I remember was Stalbridge, and our last station was Poole. We had to leave the train there and go on to Bournemouth light engine, clean the fire, turn the engine and fill it up with water and then have something to eat. When we first started from Bath we should have left at 1.00am which meant I started work at 11.30pm the previous evening. We arrived at Bournemouth about 7.00am which meant I had been on duty for 7¹/₂ hours without a rest. As it was wartime, food was scarce and you could not get anything to eat. We had to go back to Poole, then we went as a pilotman to Dorchester South where we picked up a troop train with British troops and took them to Bath where they continued their journey north. We got back at 11.00am in the morning. It was a long day and we were absolutely whacked, especially when we were working on an empty stomach.

In wartime the wives of railwaymen had a lot to put up with. They never knew when we were coming home and they had quite a job finding food for us to take to work. We had special rations which was just a little bit of cheese; it was only through them that some of us kept going.

One experience I recall was also in wartime. I was a driver on an American ambulance train with LNER stock on. This stock had a different braking system than on the LMS and it took some getting used to. We picked this train up at Bath Green Park; it was a double header. Ernie Hemmings was the driver on one of the engines and I was the driver on the leading engine assisting him. We stopped at various stations to take off the wounded and eventually arrived at our destination at Bailey Gate where American ambulances were waiting to ferry the soldiers to hospitals in the area. Unfortunately pulling into Bailey Gate we had a slight snatch, we must have used the brake a little bit fiercely, because if you knocked the vacuum brake back too many inches then your brake would suddenly go on, a feature of this type of braking system. When eventually we stopped, the captain in charge of the train came up to the footplate and gave us a real verbal hammering. He told us: "Didn't we know we had seriously wounded troops on board?" Of course we apologized and we were very sorry but we couldn't help it. We did not do much damage as we were only going very slowly but it was an experience that really upset us.

1936

George Tucker – Driver

I started on the S&D on 8th August 1936 as an engine cleaner. I passed for firing after three months and in 1941 became a passed fireman. The rapid promotion came because of the war years. When I started my firing duties many of the old time drivers were great to work with. I remember one amusing incident with Walt Warren who was always immaculately turned out. Walt was in the pit oiling up at No 2 road at Bath Green Park. He put the oil feeder can on the edge of the pit but as he was making his way out of the pit the can fell over and covered him in oil. He got out of the pit and in temper threw the oil can on the floor. The oil spurted up and covered his face again in oil. Then he started jumping on the can squashing it to the ground.

Another time was not so funny. We had a spell of very bad weather which I think was in 1947. I booked on around 10.30pm for a spare turn of duty on the shed; my driver at that time was Osmond Pitt. Some time after midnight we were instructed by the supervisor to relieve driver Edgar Gray who had just returned from a trip to Shepton Mallet with the snow plough attached to a side tank engine, the driver jokingly making the remark: "It's a waste of time, there's little drifting." We set off from Bath, having an uneventful trip as far as Masbury. There must have been inclement weather before this night because of Masbury signalbox being open. Normally it was only a day shift box. All communication between Masbury and Shepton Mallet was lost so we were sent forward by the signalman, Harry Hovey. On the time interval system he allotted us 30 minutes to arrive at Shepton Mallet, take water and clear the section before letting another train in. Now this is where the trouble started. We proceeded from Masbury, but on approaching the cutting before Winsor Hill Tunnel we started to slow up. This was caused by drifting snow. Although we were on a falling gradient, my driver started to open the regulator but it was useless and we eventually came to a standstill with the snow up to the top of the water tank. All our efforts to free ourselves from this drift failed. As stated previously, being on the time interval system, another train would soon be entering the section. I walked through the snow to protect the line armed with detonators and red flags but had great difficulty in walking. In these conditions you lost track of time because I was amazed to see an approaching train, the 2.40am mail from Bath. I managed to stop this train with about a $1/4$ mile to spare. I returned to my own engine for a warm and a can of tea and shortly after a gang of platelayers arrived to dig us out. The snow they were removing was being piled up on the up line, so I walked to the entrance of Winsor Hill Tunnel to protect this obstruction. The ganger, questioning my action, was trying to assure me that no train would be leaving Shepton Mallet. So much for unwritten instructions because shortly after turning my back to return to my engine three detonators that I had just laid exploded, caused by a light engine being sent in; a lucky escape for everybody.

Stanier 8F, No 48706, at the entrance to Norton Hill Colliery with George Tucker (left), fireman David Norman in the cab and guard Bill Parrett. (G.Tucker collection)

Another time when firing to Osmond we had pulled out from Evercreech Junction sidings with 35 wagons on and backed onto five more with the guards van on the rear. Now on the S&D there were various types of guards. One type we liked was called the percentage guard so named because he put more overtime in your pocket by making the jobs last longer. Coming out of the siding I said to Osmond: "How many should we have on?" and he replied "about 40". I said: "There is more than that I'm sure." As we pulled round the corner and looked back, we couldn't believe what met our eyes; there were 15 wagons tied on the back of the brake van. We still kept going and finally made Evercreech New, where we took the 15 wagons off. That took us another 45 minutes which caused us to cross another train at Midford and this put another hour on our time card and extra money in our wages.

I remember working the 2.40 mail from Bath Green Park to Bournemouth, which was a lodging turn. This particular driver and myself should have gone into lodgings but instead we used to go to the pictures where the driver would give the attendant 6d to wake us up. We would see the start of the film, go to sleep then see the start of the film again. Before going to the pictures we used

A BR Standard class 4 2-6-0 crosses Midford Viaduct with a Bath train. Notice the Austin Cambridge Farina saloon on the left and that the Hope and Anchor *pub still kept Simonds ales. (D.Walden collection)*

to have a couple of pints and then off to the British restaurant (a wartime project introduced by the government) for a three-course meal. The waitress would ask if you wanted soup as a starter but the old driver would say: "Don't worry about that love, we've had our soup down the local *Railway Inn*".

Another amusing incident that I recall was with driver Charles Hamilton. Friday night we would be coupled to a down passenger train to Bournemouth West and bring up the Pines Express on Saturday. We would always have a good night out in Bournemouth. On one occasion we came across some party hats. On the Pines next day Charles put a hat on when running into Bath. The chargeman at that time was Tom White. Unfortunately he had witnessed this and when we got into the shed Tom came up to Charles and said: "What do you think this is, the ruddy Palladium show?"

During the late 1950s we worked a relief train to the Pines Express. This was a regular occurrence, passenger traffic being very heavy especially during the summer holiday period. This particular day I was assisted (being over the load) with a class 2 passenger engine, with a Templecombe crew on the footplate. On approaching Writhlington the distant signal was in the off position. We were just passing under the home signal when I heard the signal crash back to the on position (some signalmen would be rather eager and do this too early). I also state the Templecombe men didn't notice this and looked back to query my braking, as they had passed the signal. My first reaction was to brake, also keeping my eye on the starting signal just in case the signalman had made a mistake. As it turned out he had not and the starter was on. Grinding to a halt just past the signalbox, the signalman was hanging out of his signalbox waving a red flag and pointing in our forward direction. There on the farm crossing was a broken-down tractor with a mountain of hay. Thinking about this later I could just picture this wrapped around the smokebox of the assisting engine.

I liked working the class 7Fs but a point to mention about this class of locomotive is that they would wear out a set of cast-iron brake blocks every other trip. They then introduced Ferodo brake blocks especially designed to fit the class 7. One day when Osmond and myself were on 7F No 53801 we had two extra people on the footplate, a loco inspector and one from Ferodo, with another person from Ferodo in the guards van. We left Bath Green Park at about 11.00am to test these brakes which had been fitted to our engine. When braking a bit heavy on greasy and wet days these brakes had a tendency for the wheels to pick up and very often they would be slow in releasing and you would soon get flats in the tyres. As we left Bath Green Park, Osmond said to me: "I'll give them Ferodo blocks today" thinking he was going to get these wheels to pick up. They would do anything but that on this particular morning and when we reached Evercreech Junction the Ferodo people became really upset. On inspection of the brake blocks the bottom part had broken off three of them. After this journey the whole block was redesigned and introduced on all class 7s on the S&D.

After all these years some of us who worked on the old Dorset still have a natter about our Bath Green Park days. Nice to remember what was, for us, a great time with great mates.

1938

Freda Box – Crossing Keeper

My late husband Fred and myself became the crossing keepers at Bruton Road, near Evercreech, in November 1938. It was not an easy existence, especially with three children to bring up; no running water, no electricity, no gas, our lights were paraffin lamps and warmth was a coal fire. Our water was delivered in five-gallon cans by train. If the crew were a friendly bunch, as most were, like drivers and firemen Archie Gunning, Bill Rawles, David Massey and Ron Bean, not forgetting guards Frank Staddon, Frank Packer, Reg Brewer and Dickie Bird, they would supplement our coal ration with some extra coal off the tender. In the garden we had a large wooden butt for rainwater which we used for washing. We had an allotment in the garden which kept the family in fresh vegetables.

Fred and I worked 24 hours a day between us, seven days a week. We had a break from the crossing in the war years when Fred was called up. We spent 25 years at Bruton Road. What amazed us was when we had a short holiday, the powers that be sent three men to work the gates over the 24 hour period.

We had a small hut next to the cottage where the wheel was kept. I used to count how many winds it took to manoeuvre the signal; it was in fact 20 and over 25 years it must have run into thousands. It couldn't have done me any harm as I'm now in my 80s and I could still do it today (once).

I do recall one dark night being frightened out of my skin. I was in the hut winding up the signal when there was an almighty shout, then a clatter of metal followed by groaning. I gingerly came out of the hut and went over to the roadway carrying a Tilley lamp. Sprawled across his bicycle was one of the Evercreech Junction signalmen on his way home. Unfortunately he had consumed too much scrumpy at the *Railway Hotel* and had fallen off his bike

Bruton Road crossing with the keeper's cottage. Note the fine array of S&D warning and trespass signs. (D.Milton)

into the ditch. He apologized for frightening me and brushed himself down. He got back on his now twisted bicycle and wobbled up the lane to his home. This was a regular occurrence with this signalman who did enjoy his drink.

Summer Saturdays were very busy. It was lovely to see the Pines Express roaring through with its happy holidaymakers going to Bournemouth, with such drivers as Donald Beale, Peter Smith, Eric Elford, Johnny Walker and Ron Gray giving a friendly wave. We always thought we were doing our bit at the crossing for this most famous express; when we travelled on it we thought we were royalty.

I remember in late 1962, when the snow was nearly as high as the crossing gates, the children and ourselves moved heaps of snow off the track to try and make sure we kept the crossing open. The engine with its snow plough would be coming up and down the track to keep the trains moving; we made sure that the crew had hot steaming cups of tea in their fight against the elements.

One busy summer Saturday nearly turned to tragedy. Fred was going to Bruton to get some shopping and we had locked the gates as an express was due. One of my sons, seeing his dad on the other side of the gate, wanted to join him. He somehow opened the wicket gate and was about to run across the track. I just managed to grab him and pull him away as the train hurtled through – what a fright. With one daughter, Jean, and two boys, Gerald and David, it was always a worry bringing up a young family with trains going by a matter of yards from our front door. You always had to be vigilant.

I hated going on the crossing when it was thundering and lightning. Also some people got angry when they were kept waiting if I didn't open the gates quickly. Many times the Evercreech Junction stationmaster, Mr Jack Pike, would phone up to say the huntsman and his hounds were on the move and we had orders to stop the trains and let them through.

One wartime memory that I shall always remember is this. Fred and myself were waiting for the bell to ring to open the crossing gates for a train. We could hear a plane in the distance, getting lower and lower. It seemed to be circling the crossing out of control. A British bomber suddenly veered off, bringing down telephone wires, and then we heard a loud explosion in the distance. Fred found someone with transport and drove quickly to Evercreech Junction and told the stationmaster who in turn got in touch with Templecombe in case the plane had crashed on the line. Some time later a train stopped at the crossing. The pilot of the bomber got off and asked in what direction the plane had crashed. He explained that he and four of his crew had bailed out safely after the plane got into difficulties. During the night RAF personnel came to guard the bits of the plane that were left. Being wartime, no one was allowed to photograph the scene.

In 25 years at the crossing we only had one accident. One morning a passenger train went through and we knew that a light engine would be following. Unfortunately we only opened two of the four gates because of a crisis in the cottage. All of a sudden we heard a bang that was the class 2P engine knocking the gates down. We rushed outside and apologized to the crew. We thought we would lose our jobs but we only got a slight ticking off.

We met many S&D people who would pass the crossing or come in for a chat and a cup of tea, people like Les Williams, Vic Freak, Ken Atkins, Joe Kemp, Arthur Francis, Tom Ashman, Frank Padfield and our dear friends at Lamyatt crossing, Norman and Mary Lockwood.

Fred and I thought the railway would never close. Bruton Road crossing was our home and life, and we opened those gates in all types of weather – wind, rain and snow. Now Dr Beeching was kicking us out. When we closed those gates in 1966 for the last time, tears were in our eyes, it was goodbye to our S&D friends. The only way of life we had known was at an end.

Bruton Road painting gang prepare to repaint the gates with help from Mrs Box's children. (F.Box collection)

1939

Arthur King – Driver

One amusing story I remember was when I was a fireman on the S&D in the 1940s. My driver and I were sent to Templecombe to work a special to Bath. On arrival we walked to the lower platform to relieve a Templecombe crew. Our guard, the well-liked Frank Staddon, went to the toilet leaving his kit and hand lamp on the platform. His lamp was lit as it was dark. It was a Western type and must have been one of the first ones on the S&D. Nearby a box of fish had broken open on the platform and my mate picked up three of the fish and lifted up the top of Frank's lamp which was hinged for cleaning. He put the fish inside the lamp. On the way to the loco shed Frank's lamp kept going out and he couldn't understand why. When we arrived at the messroom Frank lit his lamp again and turned it up as high as he could. It was not long before the fish started frying. What a smell! The messroom emptied at once, leaving Frank to examine his handlamp. Frank took it all in good fun and we all had a good laugh about it for many a day.

Ivatt class 2 2-6-2 tank, No 41307, heads into platform three at Templecombe in June 1965 with one Bulleid coach, one Great Western coach and one Southern B van. (D.Walden)

The S&D men based at Bath not only worked to Evercreech, Templecombe and Bournemouth but also over the Midland railway to Bristol, Birmingham and Derby. One day I was on a spare turn at Bath and was informed that I was going to Gloucester to work a coal train to Westerleigh, then light engine back to Bath. I relieved this train at Tramway Junction and the first thing I did was to put my brake clip on. This was a device used by S&D drivers for use over the Mendips to save water in the boiler. It was made out of a large split pin and was shaped to fit in the brake lever guide, then bent to fit in front of the fulcrum lever on the brake valve. This held the brake right off. As you can guess this was illegal to use. It meant you now had no brake until the clip was taken off. Once it was taken off the small ejector could be opened again.

I left Tramway Junction and was going slowly through Gloucester Eastgate station when who should jump on but Midland inspector Jack Dowell. He saw the brake clip and said "you can take that off", which I did and put it in my pocket. He rode with us to Bath and no more was said about the clip. Two days later I had the same turn, but this time I was not going to get caught so I would not put the clip on until I had left Gloucester. Going through the station inspector Dowell got on again. We had a class 4 engine and it was not doing at all well, short of steam and water. Mr Dowell looked at me and said: "Haven't you got your brake clip?" I replied "yes" and he said: "I should put it on if I were you." I couldn't win, could I?

1940

Bernard Kilmister – Driver

On 12th April 1940 I joined the S&D as an engine cleaner at Bath Green Park. My wage was 32/6 and the hours were from 7.00am until 3.30pm with a half hour for dinner. Many good friendships started here in the sheds which have lasted to this day. Sometimes when you arrived at work you had to take turns to clean the office floor on your hands and knees; this took some scrubbing as so much oil was walked in from the shed but it was religiously carried out each day, which I never understood as within a few minutes it was black again.

One Thursday a few of the top railway brass from Derby came to inspect the depot. From my position in the shed I was able to look out onto the ashpit where half a dozen of the older cleaners were loading a wagon with ashes. Among them was a fellow named Jocky Bullock. He was always game for a laugh and noticing that these men from Derby were on the other side of this wagon, all smartly dressed, Jocky lifted a large shovelful of ashes and taking accurate aim threw the whole lot right over the top, right in the middle of them. You can imagine the pandemonium, one went down on the oily ground, two others lost their bowler hats. Of course no one found out who carried it out as all the lads disappeared, but this was a topic of conversation in the messroom for many years after.

Some weeks went by and about a dozen of us were on the late shift from 6.00pm till 2.30am. Some of the lads I recall were Danny Levi, Ernie Hobbs, Arthur Derrick, Ralph Holden, Albert Wilcox, Edgar Smith, Cyril Beale, Ken Norris, Reg Staddon and Sid White. After about 18 months of cleaning, some of us were promoted to passed cleaners which meant that we could be called upon at any time to fire engines on the main line. As I had a lot of interest in the railway I joined mutual improvement classes which were held on Sunday mornings, when the older and more experienced hands gave lectures free. Some of them I remember were Norman Rosenburg, Len West and Arthur Turner.

It was in the winter of 1942; the main office was being altered and quite a number of tongued and grooved planks had been removed. It was the practice that if you wanted anything like that you had to put in a claim form, which I did. Over a week went by and eventually I had permission to remove some. The following week I was on late shift in the shed. I was on my own cleaning in almost total darkness and over and over in my mind was how could I get this wood home as I lived two miles away. Wandering from the shed I found myself on the bridge by the loco signal and it suddenly occurred to me, why not use the evening freight to Westerleigh. Without a second thought I went back to where I had bundled up the wood and struggled with it up onto the bridge. The freight train was just backing onto the rear portion and I noticed that a low crocodile wagon was not far from the front. Still struggling I managed to put the wood onto it and climb on myself; the train moved on its way. When it was getting near Bath Junction box I could see the signalman looking at each wagon in turn as it passed by. So as not to be seen I got down low in the wagon, so much so that my coat was rubbing the front wheel axle. Looking back I could see that I had not been noticed. The train was now picking up speed but as a passed cleaner who had fired an engine I wasn't unduly worried By the time we were approaching Weston station (about a mile from Bath), where I intended to throw off the wood, the speed I estimated was about 30mph. On reaching the platform I heaved the wood onto it. Quickly going over to the other side of the wagon I picked a spot in the dark and jumped onto the opposite track, rolling over as I did so. I waited for the train to pass before going back to pick up the wood. Within a few minutes I had put it into our garden shed which was not far from the station. From there I ran down the road to the bus stop where a bus soon came which took me back to Bath Loco whereupon I slipped back into the shed unnoticed and resumed my cleaning duties. I had not been more than 45 minutes away from work and my point in telling this story is that to this day my wife uses a very strong wooden ironing board that I made from the Bath Green Park office's firewood.

When I was firing we worked the 11.00am freight train to Evercreech Junction and on one particular day we had a class 7. Its number in those days was 13802. Having shunted the train off at Evercreech we turned the engine on the turntable, made a cup of tea on the footplate and ate our sandwiches. When the signal came off we left the table and arrived in the up goods yard. Our load was 40 empties for Midsomer Norton. On the way we had to stop at Chilcompton to pick up three wagons for Bath. We set off and duly arrived at Chilcompton. As we were coming to a standstill at the signalbox the signalman put down his knitting and told us that there was nothing to pick up so we made our way on to Midsomer Norton. When we were between Chilcompton and Midsomer Norton I looked back and saw that our brake van was not on the back of the train. I immediately informed the driver Arthur Turvy who seemed very worried. When we reached Norton he went up into the signalbox to explain the position. The signalman informed the driver that his guard had uncoupled his brake van for the three wagons at Chilcompton and we had left him behind. It was arranged that as the gradient from Chilcompton was 1:50, the guard could release his brake on the van and coast into Midsomer Norton which he did. Once he arrived we coupled up and left immediately for Bath. The management never heard a word about it, but it must have looked funny to anyone who saw the van gliding into Midsomer Norton station on its own.

BR Standard class 4 tank, No 80146, working hard as it passes Chilcompton signalbox with a four-coach train in June 1965. (R.E.Toop)

2P, No 40634, pilots West Country Braunton, No 34046, with a Bournemouth train out of Chilcompton tunnel. The spectators seem to have ignored the trespass sign by the road. (R.E.Toop)

One Saturday afternoon in June in the 1940s I was booked with driver Charlie Brown to work a "pigeon special" to Christchurch. Our guard was Larry Maggs. We came on duty at 2.10pm and collected our class 4 engine, No 4558. We left the loco shed at 3.20pm for Bath station, coupled to eight vans of pigeons (224 tons) and at 3.45pm we left, took the single-line tablet at Bath Junction and climbed out of the city. Charlie, a freight man for many years, kept altering the controls as he couldn't make his mind up in what position to leave the regulator and reverser. He seemed out of touch with this type of train. We went through the Devonshire and Combe Down tunnels, I gave up the tablet at Midford with no trouble, and we went on our way to Radstock. With the distant signal off we started to climb the $8\frac{1}{2}$ miles to the Mendip hills and on reaching the top we started to coast down the other side. Our speed increased quite significantly. It appeared Charlie wasn't used to this as when we were approaching Winsor Hill he put the brake on so hard that the train came to a complete standstill. Getting the vacuum back with the help of the large ejector we started off again, going through Shepton Mallet with enough speed to take us up over a short hill and down the other half of the Mendips, a distance of about four miles. Arriving at Evercreech Junction we took water and Charlie said: "We've done well lad, we're on time." Leaving Evercreech it was just a matter of keeping the steam and water up until we reached Templecombe where we took the single-line tablet for Stalbridge, exchanged again for Sturminster Newton and then again for Shillingstone and onto Blandford, where we gave up the tablet and came onto double lines. About five miles on, Charlie started to blow the whistle before we got to a farm crossing called Green Lane. Slowing down, Charlie called out to the gatekeeper: "See you George when we come back." On we went to Corfe Mullen, took the tablet for the single line, climbed the hills for about two miles before we dropped down to Broadstone. The tablet was given up, and still going downhill we approached Poole and went into the freight yard. Arriving at the end of the road we were met by the shunter who informed us that the train was terminating there so after uncoupling we went light engine to Branksome shed to turn the engine before going back to Bath. Charlie said to me: "Go into the messroom and make some tea." We had our tea and sandwiches and within half an hour we left the shed light engine for Bath. As we were approaching Green Lane crossing Charlie started to blow the whistle again, stopping the engine just clear of the gates. He said: "Go on the tender lad and throw some coal off." This I did and about half a ton later Charlie came out of the crossing keeper's house with two parcels. "Right lad, that's enough," and off we went like a bullet. Going between Blandford and Shillingstone he opened the smaller of the two parcels and said to me: "Look at these lovely eggs" (you could only get them in powder form in the wartime). I replied: "Yes, I haven't had an egg for some time." We eventually got to Bath and booked off. In the lobby Charlie said: "Goodnight lad, you did really well." I replied: "Goodnight Charlie, enjoy your eggs."

On the notice board one day there was a note asking men to see whether they wanted to be fire watchers or join the Home Guard. I decided with a mate of mine, Ron Shearn, to join the Home Guard. This was in June 1943. We were kitted out with a uniform and looked the part. One Sunday we were marched to a place called Hampton Rocks, a small isolated beauty spot on a hill east of Bath. We were told that each of us in turn had to throw a live grenade overhand as close to a small bush as possible. We were all told to get down in what looked like a large bomb crater covered in grass. I had settled on the top rim of the hole where there was a lot of gravel. Each of us in turn went forward to throw a grenade and on the word of command the grenade was thrown. I looked back down the pit and could see everyone with their heads buried in the grass. As the bomb went off I threw a large handful of gravel up into the air and you could hear it tinkle on their helmets. This went on for quite some time to such an extent that some of the men requested that they be moved back further. I couldn't stop laughing. One of the Bath Green Park men, Dennis Clem, was about to throw a grenade. He had pulled out the pin and dropped it. As there was a four-second fuse, Sergeant Gordon King shouted "run for it". Of course we did not need telling twice. About 30 seconds later the grenade still had not gone off. Fortunately for everyone a fuse had not been fitted, a lucky escape .

I recall a wartime firing turn with driver Dick Windsor, coming on duty at 8.50am. We were late off shed owing to the lack of a pricker rod; eventually one was found in the blacksmith's. We had a class 2 engine and we were off to Bournemouth which was a lodging turn. Getting to Bath Green Park station we were coupled to a special inspection coach with none other than Harry Whitaker on board (whose father Alfred designed the single-line tablet apparatus). Mr Whitaker came up to the engine and said I had not brushed some sand off the engine. The amount I cleared up would not have filled a thimble. Off we set at 10.00am with our one coach and the dignitary on board. We had to stop at every station to Evercreech Junction allowing Mr Whitaker and others to meet the staff and look around the stations. We arrived at Evercreech and then proceeded tender first to Highbridge and Burnham-on-Sea. On the way we took water at Glastonbury. Mr Whitaker came out of the coach and asked me: "Is the water smelly"? I replied, "yes," and he said: "What a pity, it's always been like this as the water is drawn from the peat bogs." We arrived at Burnham-on-Sea station which was built right next to the sandy beach. It was quite an experience to see the sea a few yards away. After half an hour we headed back non-stop to Evercreech, exchanging tablets all the way. Again Mr Whitaker and company had a talk to the Evercreech Junction stationmaster. This same procedure went on all the way to Broadstone where we came onto the Southern Railway. We then made a non-stop trip to Bournemouth West arriving at 5.00pm. We lodged at Branksome with driver Johnny Walker and his wife who made us very welcome. Next morning we took the same engine, No 697, and left for Bath again with the inspection coach and Mr Whitaker. We took water at Blandford Forum whilst Mr Whitaker carried out his inspection of the station. We then went through Shillingstone, and going through Sturminster Newton at speed we had to give and take the token together. For some reason the Whitaker apparatus failed. We managed to take the token for Stalbridge but the token for Sturminster got hit from the catcher apparatus and went up into the air and landed in a flower bed on the platform. Dick put the brake into an emergency stop and we came to a standstill about a quarter of a mile on, where I got off the footplate and ran back to the signalbox. The signalman by this time was halfway down the platform looking for the tablet. He put his arm up into the air when he found it to indicate for us to proceed. On arrival into Bath an official jumped from the coach and gave Dick 5/– and myself 2/6 with the words, "well done".

When the 44-hour working week came in I was put into a regular link with driver Tom Gunning. I must say it was a treat to come to work as Tom was a very considerate man. This kept me in good stead right through my S&D career which sadly finished when we were closed down in March 1966.

1940

Reg Darke – Driver

Leaving Templecombe school at the age of 14 I wanted to work on the S&D like my father, grandfather and great grandfather who were all S&D drivers. Unfortunately I couldn't because in those days you had to be 17 years of age before you could join the S&D.

In those three years I had eight various jobs, having to cycle or walk many miles. I worked for W H Smith at Templecombe Upper bookshop in this period before the war. We sold hundreds of newspapers, the popular ones being 1d each. The S&D was really hectic, with the busiest time during the early hours of summer Saturday mornings. Many factories in the North and the Midlands closed down for their summer holidays. These factories ran their own special trains to Bournemouth. Two special trains I well remember were for the Leicester Co-op and John Player & Sons of Nottingham. Some of the Bath drivers who drove these specials were Bill Amos, Sam Randall, Bill Lee, Bert Lee (my uncle) and Bill Nicholls.

I finally started on the S&D on 30th December 1940 as a cleaner at Templecombe. It was not too long, because of the war conditions, before I became a fireman. My first trip as a fireman was with driver Jack Loader. We were on a local train to Wincanton on a Wednesday which was market day. We loaded cattle as they were sold and herded them from the nearby market to our train. We also loaded milk from the local factory (the home of Cow & Gate) and then worked to Templecombe Upper goods yard where our train was transferred to the Waterloo SR line. I remember our locomotive for this journey was a 4F, No 4557.

In 1941 the up Pines Express was always manned by Templecombe crews, the first crew working the 7.15 Templecombe to Bournemouth, returning with the 9.45 Pines to Stalbridge where they were relieved by our second crew. The down Pines was worked throughout by Bath Green Park men and called at Templecombe Upper, arriving at 3.30pm.

Reg Darke leans out of the cab of 4F, No 44560, at Templecombe. (D.Walker)

My first trip on this train was a difficult one. I was still only working on freight trains. When I booked on duty the foreman called me into his office looking very worried. He informed me that he had to use fireman Bill Goddard as a driver on another train and I was the only one available for the Pines. He said: "I can't be sure that driver Sams will take you." When the driver booked on he was most annoyed at having to take out the youngest kid in the depot; he said very little travelling to Stalbridge. The Pines ran in with a 4F freight engine. The next stop was Evercreech Junction and after leaving here Ernie Sams spoke to me for the first time saying: "My lad, I would like you to be my mate all the time." I was taken aback by this remark as we hadn't done the slog up to the Mendips. I had many more trips with Ernie Sams. One morning we were fortunate to survive. We were at Evercreech Junction shunting our train off into the up sidings when shunter Ned Ashman held up a red flag. As we were stationary at the time this puzzled me until suddenly a large black plane came out of the clouds and seconds later came the explosions. A Heinkel bomber had bombed Castle Cary station destroying the signalbox and turning a locomotive over in the yard, killing some railwaymen and also civilians in nearby cottages. Why they attacked there and left the large marshalling yard at Evercreech alone we will never know. We now knew the red flag meant an air raid warning.

Templecombe was mainly involved with freight trains made up of war materials, ammunition, petrol and of course troop and hospital trains. When Americans were stationed here we had to take a freight train that took us off the S&D. We booked on duty at 3.15pm with a class 7F engine and would go tender first to Highbridge Wharf and work heavy petrol trains to Hamworthy in Dorset. The class 7F engines were not normally used on the branch line and were restricted to a slow speed owing to the marshy track base. All the single-line tokens were exchanged by hand. If red alert air raid warnings occurred we were stopped at the next passing point, with the firebox shut tight and no steam allowed to escape. If it did the local air raid warden would be on the warpath. These trains were the beginning of many trips over the Broadstone to Hamworthy Junction single line where we crossed the main Poole to Weymouth line to Hamworthy Quay into an American base.

The war also brought many women into the S&D ranks who were excellent at their jobs. I recall the signalwoman at West Pennard, Mrs Evelyn Curtis. She had her special mark on the platform to show where to stand when exchanging the single-line token. We knew we needed a reasonable speed to ascend Pylle bank. Some signalmen would get nervous exchanging the tablet but Mrs Curtis would stand unflinching to collect the token, a brave lady indeed. She also kept her signalbox filled with a nice array of plants.

January 20th was an unforgettable day, the reason being that I saved a life and lost a life. On this Saturday in 1945 I was a fireman on the day tripper which was two freight train trips from Templecombe Upper yard to Evercreech Junction. On the second trip we arrived at 1.55pm at Evercreech Junction North home signal at danger. Our locomotive was 7F No 53810. The head shunter, Alec Fear, was shunting a train in the 'Neck' siding which was the line that went round the rear of the signalbox. Meanwhile the under shunter came across and uncoupled our engine from the train, the signal came off and he waved my driver Bert Jones forward to cross over onto the turntable road. I was leaning out of my side when I just caught sight of half a hand moving up and down in front of the engine. There was no time to shout stop, I just dived across the footplate and knocked the steam brake handle across and slammed the regulator shut. Bert looked round at me puzzled, so I pointed a shaking finger out the front, fearing the worst. Fortunately Alec appeared unharmed, he had been so intent on catching the shunting driver's eye behind the signalbox that he had been unaware that he had been about three seconds from death or serious injury. Later that day the village policeman knocked on our door to tell us father was seriously ill in Bristol Royal Infirmary and to go there at once. That evening father passed away.

I cannot recall many unusual experiences as a fireman; like everyone else I had good trips and also bad ones. We tolerated some very rough locomotives but as long as they steamed freely we were happy with that. After the war the Pines Express was worked by Branksome crews. On one occasion I had to travel to Bournemouth to work this train to Bath with driver Alec Bolwell. We had a Black Stanier LMS class engine. I thought my luck was in, as usually when we went to Branksome to help out we more often than not had a 4F LMS freight engine. What a trip! On the tender there was not a lump of coal to be seen, just a ton of slack. We struggled to Stalbridge where we had lost some time but good driving by Alec enabled us to coast down Shepton Montague bank to Evercreech Junction where by the time the assisting engine had coupled up we were in much better shape and were right on time into Bath Green Park.

Radstock North in July 1964. Standard class 4, No 75007, is about to cross the road and enter the station with a Bournemouth to Bristol train. A Bristol LS bus bound for Wells waits at the crossing gate while the signalman's bicycle rests beneath the stairs to his box. (D.Walden)

Another trip I recall was on the night Poole freight train. This train left Bath at 5.15pm, working all intermediate stations including Evercreech Junction. We relieved the Green Park crew in Templecombe Lower yard and on this occasion we had a locomotive inspector riding with us because of the time being regularly lost on the return train from Poole. This was due to a dirty fire in most cases, but they were trying to blame the train crews for losing running time. The inspector informed us he would be doing the firing coming back. The driver looked across and beckoned me over to whisper: "I think we'll see some fun tonight." My driver was Bert Jones, rather a quiet and reserved man but one of the most brilliant enginemen on the S&D. As well as being an excellent driver he knew the rule book from A to Z and his knowledge of the various locomotives was second to none. He was a strong trade unionist and a very good cricketer in his younger days. On the return trip we were on a 7F freight train with 55 wagons; the inspector, complete with overalls, took over the shovel. As Bert had already foreseen, before many miles had been covered he was looking at the steam gauge. Unbelievably he called across to Bert: "I think you had better stop, driver." Bert replied: "I shan't be stopping, I have been in more dire straits than this." At Blandford, while taking water, the inspector was slogging away to raise the steam pressure as it was a hard climb to the top of Milldown. Nearing Shillingstone I asked him if he would like to put the single-line tablet in the catching apparatus but he didn't fancy that task. Eventually we crawled over Templecombe Junction with 110 lbs of steam pressure which was quite average as anything over 90 lbs was reasonable. Our inspector was supposed to come with us for the week but strangely we never saw him again.

The day I shall never forget was assisting the up Pines Express with a 3F freight engine, No 3444. The booked class 2 passenger loco had been used for a military train and control was sending 3444 in from Evercreech Junction for coaling and watering for our assisting duty. Our trip light engine to Evercreech Junction was normal and we coupled to the express. Leaving Evercreech we noticed the exhaust blast was a shade noisier than usual. These locomotives were nicknamed Bulldogs because of the bark out of their chimney. Everything

Standard class 4 2-6-4T, No 80147, enters Shillingstone going north with a mixed rake of coaches. Note the unusual telegraph pole. The down shelter looks as if it was placed there that day. The rundown has begun – the remains of the platform lamp and the unattended tub look forlorn. (E.Rimmer)

went normally up the Mendips and over the top at Masbury Summit, passing through Chilcompton, we entered the tunnel. We came out the other end and, knowing my driver was unsighted due to the track curvature, I looked out of my side window for the up distant signal for Midsomer Norton. Seeing it was clear I shouted "right away" to the driver, Dennis Norris. It was then I happened to look down along the side of the engine framing and noticed a huge bolt rolling around so I said to Dennis: "There's a bloody great bolt out on my side." He came across and his face paled. Dashing back he applied the brakes and we came to a stand in Norton platform. A quick inspection told us that this was our lucky day. The bolt had jumped out of the left outside slide bar or piston guides. The piston had snapped off at the rear end and was being pushed complete with piston head into the cylinder. The inside bolt was also loose so we informed the signalman. We had to detach and coast quietly down the bank to Radstock. This he would not allow and somehow we had to cross over onto the down line but we thought this was impossible on this steep gradient. We went down clear of the crossover and came to a standstill. I got off the engine and looking around the wheel I could direct my driver to position the right valve open to steam power. Remembering you had full power on the right piston only, it was no easy task to get across to the other track on this steep gradient. The amazing thing about this occurrence is that nothing was ever heard about it until now, but thank heaven that big bolt leapt up onto the engine frame and not down on the ballast as there is no doubt in my mind that opening up full power through Radstock we would have jumped the rails and that would have been fatal as we could have ploughed into shoppers in the market place or hit Kath Parker in her high signalbox. Although the driver had to report the cause of the delay before booking off duty we heard nothing more about it. What could have been a second disaster for Radstock was well hushed up. It was noticeable that 3F engines were never booked to assist this train in the up direction after this day except in emergencies, although they still assisted weekend specials from Bath.

All goods trains were loose coupled and depended on the engine brakes and the guards van brake only. Every driver who had Charlie Light as his guard from Templecombe to Poole on a fully-loaded train was judged by Charlie whether it was a good ride. Charlie would say we have two fictitious trucks of cows on today, which he called heavy cattle (of course sometimes there was). If he had any buffering or snatches in his van and if any of the cows, in his estimation, had been knocked down, that driver would get a real roasting; a true railwayman was Charlie. Between Templecombe and Blandford there were many places where the train could be on three or more different gradients at the same time. One place that comes to mind was the down line running into Shillingstone. Three gradients and a 25mph loop was an ideal place for skill testing. Running through Charlton Marshall halt there was a dip where you would get a nasty snatch. One night on the Poole goods I felt a slight one which puzzled me as the guard I had was a very conscientious man. I turned to my fireman and said: "I think our guard has nodded off." This meant a change of tactics so as not to wake him. Being a clear night and with all signals clear for us, we arrived in Poole yard. The worried guard came on the footplate and admitted he had a hot van and had dropped off to sleep.

In 1948 I was passed out as a driver by inspector Jack Dowell of Gloucester. He was well known by the footplate men for two specific reasons. If you were caught with the tender tank lid not replaced or a deflector plate not in position in the firehole mouthpiece you would find yourself reprimanded or, caught a second time, on the carpet. One piece of advice he gave me that I always kept was: "When you are in charge of a locomotive regard it as your own private property and you will not get into any serious trouble." Truer words were never spoken.

The first piece of Somerset and Dorset history I made which I was unaware of occurred on a Saturday evening. I was working a light engine to Bournemouth to work the 10.00pm train from Bournemouth West to Temple-combe Lower station. At Branksome station the signal was at danger, the signalman came down the steps and I thought: "Oh dear, something has gone wrong." He climbed up onto the footplate and said: "Do you know you are making history tonight, driver; you are the driver of the last train from Bournemouth West to work over the Somerset and Dorset." Although I knew that Bournemouth West was closing that night I never thought anything about driving the last S&D train. Normally Templecombe Lower station was our last call and if we had no passengers we ran straight to the carriage sidings, but as we were the last booked train to stop here we called just for the record book. As from the following Monday all S&D trains started from Bournemouth Central station and the 10.00pm Saturdays only was discontinued.

In 1966 when the S&D closed I went to Bristol. Before I retired in 1988 I was on an express train from Bristol to Derby. As there was no track speed above 100mph I was single manned on an HST 125 on this day. My thoughts returned to Blandford leaving with the 12.55pm Bournemouth to Bath passenger train. This train was booked to connect at Templecombe with the Brighton to North Devon train known as the Devon Belle. Passengers were allowed three minutes to cross the footbridge to catch this train which the Southern would not hold for us if we were late. On this day we had a class 2 passenger engine with a high tender and a double door which you could clamber up through when the coal was well back. I had an agile young fireman named Mervyn Belbin. After taking on water and securing the flexible pipe to the water column I scrambled back onto the footplate to release the brakes as we had already had right of way from the guard. Expecting Mervyn to appear through the tender doors I opened up the power. Glancing round the door I realised he was not there and looking back at the train, there he was looking out of the first coach window. To stop would have caused much delay so I motioned him to get in out of sight. What I at first intended to do was to stop at the top of Milldown bank and get him back then but I thought that would cause too much time lost so I carried on to Shillingstone, the next stop. What had happened was that after I had tethered the water column pipe and gone back up on the footplate, Mervyn had gone to the staffroom for a drink of water without telling me. The dear lady passengers who had been to Blandford shopping were highly amused to have the train fireman sat with them in the carriage. If any platform staff knew about that episode they kept it quiet, because like the Midsomer Norton incident I have never heard it mentioned. If anyone does recall this day may I profoundly thank you for keeping quiet because although very amusing it was a serious breach of rules. This was the only time I recall bending the rules.

I always hated running late with a passenger train. I can remember having to report once only for five minutes lost and once only for five minutes gained which was rather ridiculous.

Looking back now it was a marvellous life on the S&D working with drivers like Bill Cox, Albert Good, Charlie Cooksley and Bill Prior. Firemen I recall where Cliff Day, Keith Barrett, Mike Baker and Basil Foote, not forgetting guards George Coward, Tom Mundy, Bill Pitman and Luke Williams.

1940

Ted Lambert – Signalman

While I was working at Evercreech Junction I recall a funny incident in the 1940s. Being wartime the Somerset and Dorset railway was short of engines. Some of its locos were sent to other lines or in some cases seconded to the Army Railway Transport Unit. Replacements were sent for this loss of motive power, the Southern Region supplying some rather old class 1P 0–4–4 tank engines which had rather doubtful pulling power, so they were mostly used on the branch line between Highbridge and Evercreech Junction where the two coach sets and the passenger traffic were rather lighter for them.

Evercreech Junction staff pose happily, leaning against a train standing in the platform. The train crew are busy filling the tender with water. From left to right are Bert Baker (with the bucket), Alec Stowe, Vic Freak, George Green and Ted Lambert. (V.Freak collection)

One of these old engines struggled into Evercreech Junction one day. It arrived about 10.45am bringing in passengers who would be going in the Bath direction or down to Templecombe and along to Bournemouth. On this occasion the train came in and stopped as it usually did by the water column. The driver and fireman got down out of the cab to fill up with water. The driver, Bill Sargeant, was quite a character. Standing on the platform at the time, waiting to catch a train, was an American Army sergeant, who took a great interest in this old engine, walking up and down, viewing it and grinning to himself. He turned to Bill Sargeant and said: "Do you know what we would do with this heap of old junk, if we had it in the States?" Bill looked at him, cuffed his nose and said: "Well, I reckon you would do one of three things, you would either lean on it, chew on it or .... it." The deflated American was lost for words and left the scene quickly. Enjoying a cup of tea in the cabin later, Bill said: "That was one up for the S&D over the Americans."

1942

Norman Cook – Passed Fireman

My father, who was a driver, and brother Maurice, a fireman, were at Highbridge when I started there in 1942. Quite a few of us within a short time were passed to act as firemen as and when required. Other passed cleaners that I recall were Bill Parsons, Walt Parsons, Jim Brabner, Horace Hardridge, Jack Meaker, Ray Gibbs and Les Haines. Most of our days on the footplate were in the summertime when senior men were taking their annual holidays which were only one week per year.

As it was wartime, cleaning materials were not always available but there were many other jobs to do. Any one of us could at any time be asked to do the duties of anyone who was not actually a footplate man. We would help fitters Jack Swain and Ralph Barry, we would carry out coaling duties with George James and steamraising with Charlie Ford and Joe Ryan. Sometimes when coal was in short supply we had to load trucks from the standby coal stacks by hand. One such stack had been there for many years, the walls a credit to whoever built it. They were in fact as true and even as many brick buildings, though each piece of coal was longer and larger than concrete building blocks. However when we started to load it those large pieces of coal which had been exposed to the elements for so many years simply crumbled in our hands.

The river Brue ran behind the Highbridge locomotive works and close by was the reservoir which was kept full of water. This was pumped into our water column. At intervals one of the cleaners would be sent to the adjacent pump house to clean everything inside including the fire-fighting equipment which was stored there. One morning just before our lunch break the foreman, Bill Brady, gave me the key to the pump house and told me to spend the afternoon there cleaning everything out with strict instructions to turn the pump switch from auto to off before I did anything. Well knowing as I did that the metal cleaning paste supplied was fairly useless I borrowed my mother's tin of Brasso and secreted it in my overall pocket. After about a hour and a half's work I had every copper and brass item positively gleaming. I knew Mr Brady would come to see my progress. He first checked that I had set the switch in the off position, then looked around the pump house and almost unbelievably said that it was a credit to me that everything was gleaming. Thank goodness for mother's Brasso. On another occasion he decided that the reservoir would be much better if it had a good clean up, making sure the rushes and other vegetation were cut and removed. The water was drained out and we all set about the task which I recall lasted about three days. We found quite a few large fish, some about two feet in length. It was assumed that these were drawn in from the river when very small and had grown to their present size in a few years.

Promotion was rather slow as drivers were asked to stay on till after retirement age. However for every day which a driver worked on, the eldest passed fireman and passed cleaner would have a turn credited to him. This was due to the fact that turns counted towards one's next pay rise and 313 firing turns contributed a year's work which excluded Sundays.

We were all very keen to learn all we could about our work, particularly the engines. Many drivers like Ern Cook (my father), Bert Hansford, Bill May, Bill Peck, Harry Pearce and Charlie King would give up their Sunday mornings to attend mutual improvement classes where they would teach us about engines and also the rules and regulations. These were both important, numerous and essential to us for our work and future promotion. Those of us who were Home Guard members were let off a little earlier from Sunday parades and drilling in order to attend the classes. I always found that railwaymen both in our department and all others were generally friendly and helpful. The locomotives at Highbridge were at this time 0–4–4T and 0–6–0 3F tender engines known as Bulldogs. There were also some Southern 0–4–4Ts on loan. My favourite engines were the 0–6–0 3Fs which although rather old did years of hard work. There was also one Sentinel engine for work at Highbridge wharf.

3F, No 43216, crossing the GWR main line at Highbridge in 1960. (C.Caddy)

Often we were sent to the little depots of Bridgwater and Wells for firing duties. Another new experience at Wells was the push-and-pull train that went to Glastonbury, stopping at Polsham.

When I first worked on the Wells branch, I was shown by the driver whom I was with the water wheel which was worked by a small stream which ran alongside the engine shed. This metal wheel was operated by adjusting a vertical sluice gate so that the water could be made to run faster or slower as required. The purpose of this wheel was to pump water from the stream up to the water tank where it was subsequently used for the engines.

On reflection, in the couple of years that I worked at Highbridge I didn't realize just how much I had learnt. I became a registered fireman at Bridgwater where there was only one turn. We relieved Templecombe men at about 11.30am and worked that engine until evening during which time we worked about four passenger trips to Edington Junction and back, plus shunting the goods yard at Bridgwater and forming the goods train for the Templecombe men to take back after their rest period.

When I transferred to Bridgwater I knew there was only one shift and a six day week of 48 hours. Frequently we had two Southern locos to work with, Nos 304 and 400, both 4–4–0 tender engines, with No 400 being the slightly larger of the two. They had large driving wheels and no doubt in their prime they had worked expresses. But any pleasure that I may have had working on them was marred by the wretched firebox door. This was more or less at floor level, reasonably wide but not very deep. By pulling down on the handle the door went inwards to act as a smokeplate. If only this plate would stay horizontal then there was no problem, but the thing, whether from age, wear or whatever, just hung downwards. When cleaning the fire, which I did about midday, almost every piece of clinker would be knocked off the shovel causing some choice words on my behalf, so with poor quality coal resulting in a lot of clinker this part of the engine left much to be desired. The steam-operated reversing gear was also a poor arrangement. It would gradually slip down into full fore gear or full reverse, whichever way the loco was being driven.

Whilst waiting to relieve the Templecombe men the sound of a class 3F whistle at the distant signal would be a welcome sound. No 3248 was my favourite engine, strong, fast and rode very well.

Whilst shunting in Bridgwater yard we would sometimes stop near the stables and look out for the carter. We often saw him release the horse from the delivery cart and when this happened we would keep the engine as quiet as possible in order to hear what seemed to be a regular occurrence. The very large horse, having worked all day on the deliveries, would be led into his stable by the carter who presumably would then start to groom him. After several minutes there would be one or two loud thumps coming out of the stables. These noises were then followed by cries of rage, pain and anger from the carter. Of course we never knew what happened in the stables, but the poor man would come flying out in an awful state shouting out a variety of expletives. This happened on many occasions and gave us many laughs.

We left Edington Junction one day for Bridgwater and next to our engine was a brake third carriage which comprised several compartments with the guard's luggage compartment nearest to our tender. As we neared Cossington and entered the start of the cutting, a farmer, who was in the field above cutting cabbages, held up one of those solid vegetables to which my mate held up both hands. Well the farmer threw that cabbage as hard as he could and unfortunately the thing sailed past us and over the tender, hitting the end of the van just to the side of the window where the guard was sitting. It broke into hundreds of pieces and I saw the guard jump up in alarm. On stopping at Cossington he leapt out of the carriage and looked at the end of his van. Seeing only a wet patch, he then told us about the unknown object whilst we kept straight faces and listened incredulously to this mystery.

A well-known figure at Bridgwater was an old retired driver called Frank Braund. He was in his eighties and a very keen gardener and frequently came down to work on his allotment by the line. He would offer some little gems of information to me regarding various gardening practices and would often give me names of various seeds which I am sure were of his own making. He was a marvellous man to talk to and spent over 50 years working on the S&D. I was to think of him some years later when I left Bridgwater at the closing of the branch. We were instructed to put all items which were in our cabin into a truck to be sent away. There were lockers in that cabin but I had never seen half of what they contained (our daily duties didn't leave much spare time) so it was with some surprise when one item came to light. It was a gorky (flare lamp) and on the side of this lamp was the name, F Braund, written in solder.

Bridgwater station staff, c.1913. Note that only the dog is hatless. (D.Ashill collection)

I was passed for driving duties and whenever my mate was off for any reason it was my train to drive. By this time we were having rest days, at first every other week, then with the 40-hour week we had one every seven days.

Our trips to Edington Junction were tender-first so it was a cold and dusty ride especially in winter time. One such trip still remains vivid in my memory. It was February 4th 1947 and it was our first trip of the day. A heavy blizzard was blowing and needless to say we had put the storm sheet up but snow, as it will, blew in through the sides completely covering us. We were not aware at that time that weeks of such weather would follow. I can remember seeing a snow-covered field where a great many wild geese stayed for a long time, right opposite a little crossing house called Stone End. This was one of the two crossings where twice a week we took water for the keepers, the other one being Chilton Drove. Those poor folk had no running water, no electricity and no gas; one wonders how they survived miles from anywhere and especially in that weather.

When the Bridgwater branch trains carried a reasonable amount of passengers many of them became well known to us as they came into Bridgwater at least once per week. We always made sure there was plenty of room in the guards van for the ladies with their prams. On market days in Bridgwater quite a lot of the farming community used our trains regularly and like all the other regulars they would always wave or have a friendly chat with us. At the age of 23 I was, I suppose, very young to be passed for driving, no doubt because I was the only fireman there. I can well remember those two days with the locomotive inspector. On the first day I spent several hours learning all about engines at Highbridge motive power depot, answering many questions and naming each and every part to which he pointed. I was also asked what I would do in any eventuality and wherever possible I had to demonstrate each stage of such action. The following day I was required to go to Bath for a further medical check and a few days later the locomotive superintendent came to Bridgwater to tell me that I had passed my exam and to offer as much advice and best wishes as he could.

When the branch closed for passenger trains in 1952 I then transferred to the Western Region and a whole new way of working.

My first days at Highbridge have always stayed with me. There are many colleagues that I have never forgotten who carried out a tremendous job in supporting the footplate crew, people like the permanent way men Harry Biffin, Ernie Guy and Bert Gibbs, signal and telegraph men Tom Strike and Tom Bass. There was storeman Charlie Packer, signalmen Harry Brown, George Dewfall, crane drivers Ern Pritchard and Harry Meader and many more.

The line has now gone but is not forgotten. Highbridge can be proud of its railway history; it will stay forever in the folklore of the Somerset and Dorset Railway.

1942

Theresa Roberts (née Perry) – Booking Clerk

I was introduced to the S&D by a young man named Mick Matthews (I wonder where he is now) who was a near neighbour at Haydon, a village near Radstock, and had attended the same senior school at Midsomer Norton. Mick was already working on the S&D as a relief clerk but he was called up to go to war like so many other young men. He suggested that I apply for a job on the S&D, which I did. I joined the staff of Midsomer Norton station as a booking clerk in June 1942 in an otherwise all male environment.

As a booking clerk I worked early and late shifts on alternate weeks to cover all passenger trains, the early shift starting at 7.30 am and the late turn at 10.00am. The first train of the day was the 7.00am off Bath coming in at 7.38am taking with it the previous day's takings in a leather cash bag, which we deposited in a safe in the guards van. It was a busy station in the 1940s, with lots of passengers, parcels, goods traffic and many coal trains serving the local collieries which surrounded the district. An important part of my duties was coal truck logging to various firms on blue invoices.

I remember a farmer, Mr Hoskins of Charlton Lane Farm, ringing the station to enquire whether we could transport sugar beet that had been grown on the farm. I believe it was going to a Tate & Lyle factory somewhere in the region. Now this was a new venture for us so out came all the stops, and before long an open wagon was in the sidings. The farmer's men came into the station yard on their old tractor pulling a trailer loaded with the sugar beet, which was hand loaded into the wagon with much sweat and toil. They went backwards and forwards to the farm until the truck was fully loaded and we felt very pleased that this had been accomplished so quickly.

Theresa Roberts astride her Francis Barnett motorcycle (T.Roberts collection)

My father bought me a second-hand Francis Barnett two-stroke motorbike to get me to work. Railway work was classed as an essential service in the war so I was granted a petrol allowance, though not much as there was petrol rationing.

The atmosphere and surroundings at Midsomer Norton station were very enjoyable. As many have said before me the wonderful gardens were a pleasure to the eye and the perfume from the various flowers in bloom hung in the air on a sunny morning. You passed the garden on your right when coming into the station; the centre of the garden and the flower beds around the edge were always overflowing with blooms and the grass was cut to a fine art. Signalman Fred Griffin brought the plants on in the greenhouse next to the signalbox and whenever the porters had some spare time they could be seen pottering about in the garden. The whole staff felt a pride in their country station.

Staff there I recall were stationmasters Teddy Woods and Mr Joseph. The chief clerk was Bill Newton whose son Michael later joined us as a booking clerk; also there was porter/shunter Charlie Dowling who was a very dry Somerset chap and kept us all in fits of laughter. He used to ride very upright and slowly on his bicycle from his home at Radstock. Another of the lads at the station was porter Norman Harrison, a north country chap who used to come out with some quaint sayings, one of which I still use today: "No one is going to stop a galloping horse to look at that." Other members of the team were porters Frank Germain, Stan Jones, Herbie Cornish, clerks Bill Coomer and Bert Colbourn whom I have recently contacted after 50 years, since reading and seeing my photograph with him in Alan Hammond's previous book *Stories of the Somerset and Dorset*.

American troops were stationed on the Mendips a few miles away, prior to D-Day, and occasionally they came into the station in their trucks to pick up odd-shaped wooden crates, the contents of which we were never told. They were very sociable chaps but any friendliness was frowned upon by the stationmaster. Of course there were times when he wasn't looking which allowed me to have a chat with the American GIs.

2P, No 40696, leaving Midsomer Norton with the 1.10pm stopping train from Bath to Templecombe, with three Maunsell coaches. (R.E.Toop)

There is one sad memory that I still think about today. I was in the booking office one day when the Bath train came in and a little old lady with a very old brown suitcase got off the train looking very sad and lost. She asked us whether she could leave the suitcase with us for a while and collect it later and of course we agreed. The lady slowly made her way out of the station. The days went by, then weeks, but she never did turn up to collect it. We were all really worried and even put a little note in the Post Office window for her but this produced no response so we decided to open the case for any identification. There was not a thing in there that could help us identify her, not even a change of clothes, so we informed the police at Midsomer Norton who took all the details, but again we drew a blank. I wonder what did happen to her, and if she ever found someone to look after her, we shall never know. If only she had told us a little more of her intentions I am sure we could have helped.

When passenger trains came in I often popped out of the office to collect the tickets and of course I got to know some of the guards. One I remember particularly was Larry Maggs who, when the train was running in, would stick his head out of the guards van and call out "Ogshott, Bagshott" and other lesser-known station names. Also he would call out: "If there is anyone for here, this is it". No one seemed to notice except the station staff; he always got a good laugh from us. Another of Larry's pronouncements from the guards van was "Pouch, run round 'em". I never knew the origin of this saying but I gather it was something to do with single-line working and shunting wagons.

I was with the S&D for six years and enjoyed it very much, particularly the work and the people, but unfortunately the late shift played havoc with my social life so I decided to move on. It was a happy line even though there was a war on and it was an experience that I shall always remember.

1943

Joyce Bell (née Pearce) – Lengthwoman

My father Harry Pearce was an S&D railwayman for 50 years. He started at Bath Green Park as a call boy in 1913. He met my mum there who was an engine cleaner. They moved to Evercreech Junction where dad qualified as a driver, then on to Wells in 1923.

When we used to go on our Sunday school outing from Wells to Burnham-on-Sea I was so proud to tell my friends that my dad was driving the train. Those were the days when they used to take the engine right up to the jetty at Burnham. We used to lean out of the carriage window with our wooden windmills in our hand, they would whizz around in the wind. On our way back from the outing we used to stop at Glastonbury and dad would let my sister and myself ride on the footplate into Wells, which of course was forbidden, but I'm glad he did because it was a great thrill riding with dad on a steam engine.

Dad had an allotment at the side of the line. We used to pull out carrots and wash them under the tap in the engine shed at Wells. Carrots have never tasted as good as in those days. The line used to run along the back of our house and whenever dad took out the early train from Wells to Glastonbury he used to blow the whistle as he passed by to wake mum up. Unfortunately he used to wake the neighbours up as well!

My father was transferred to Highbridge in 1938 and we followed as soon as he found a house for us. He was a very keen and active member of the St John Ambulance and he also belonged to the S&D railway Ambulance Team. I am proud to have a letter from the St John and the Southern Region Ambulance Centre congratulating Ronald Andrews, Reg Eaton and dad for helping to save a railwayman's life in 1948.

When my dad was on the goods train to Evercreech he would stop the engine somewhere near Shapwick and put snares down to catch some rabbits. On the way back they would stop the engine and pick them up. Dad would bring them home and mum would cook us rabbit pie. He would also stop the train to pick up moon daisies for my mum. Of course he had to drive faster to make up for the lost time as no railwayman ever wanted to be late.

Drivers in conversation. Charlie King, on the platform, talks to Harry Pearce standing in the cab of a Collett 0-6-0 on his last working day in 1963. (J.Bell collection)

He once appeared on television in 1961 when the BBC filmed him on his engine taking churns of water to the crossing keepers from Evercreech to Burnham. I think it was called *The Water Run* and we all watched it on television. Dad was a heavy smoker and all the way from Evercreech he was puffing on his Woodbine.

He retired in 1963, his last train being the 2.10pm from Glastonbury into Highbridge. The S&D railway was his life. How many people can nowadays stay and enjoy their job for 50 years?

When I got married I lived in Clyce Road in Highbridge. Our garden ran down to the River Brue and the timber boats from Scandinavia used to come up to the wharf at the Town Bridge to deliver timber to Bland's timber yard. The steam engines used to shunt the trucks up to the boats. The wharf was very busy in those days. When dad was shunting on the wharf my little boy used to love to ride on the footplate with his grandpa. I also had a younger brother Reg working at Highbridge in the carriage and wagon department. He was there when the Americans were stationed there in the 1940s.

I worked on the S&D in the war years as a lengthwoman. The job consisted of clearing the weeds off the track and knocking up the ballast against the side of the line. There was a gang of ladies and Ernie Guy who was the foreman. He was a very tall man and was well respected by us. The ladies I recall were Hilda Underwood, Kit Wheadon and Phyllis Baker whose husbands George and Arthur worked on the S&D, Susie Fisher and Sally Baker, both evacuees from London (Sally had a very broad Cockney accent), Renee Ham, whose parents ran the *Rose and Crown Inn* near Highbridge station, and May Leigh.

We used to catch the 10.00am out of Highbridge station every morning and travel on the cushions to whichever length of line was allocated to us from Highbridge to Evercreech. When we arrived at the nearest station to the length of line we were working on we would always head to the gangers' hut where we would enjoy a cup of tea and a good natter. After that we would walk to the starting point of our length. We all had a pick and an iron bar which was attached to a wooden pole. The bar had one flat end and one narrow end. We then proceeded to hoe up the weeds and pull up the ballast. We were usually given a set number of lengths to do; a length consisted of an area between the joints of rail. It was extremely hard work but we enjoyed it.

In the winter time there was always a lovely fire made up of old sleepers and coal and we used to boil the old iron kettle to make a cup of tea and munch our sandwiches. In the summer months it was lovely to see the wildlife, rabbits, hares, foxes and squirrels running in between the lush green hedgerows. There were also lots of different flowers nestling close to the track. The summer also had its dangers. I can remember one time it was very hot and we were working in sleeveless tops and I suffered terrible sunburn on my arms which blistered; these burst and as we were covered in dirt from the track I ended up with septic arms and had to have two weeks off work. After our day's work we would walk back down the line, knapsack on our back; mine was an old Air Force one. I expect we looked quite a sight catching the train with our back packs.

There was a POW camp near West Pennard where the prisoners used to be allowed out to work on the farms. When they saw us girls going into the gangers' hut for our sandwiches they would come to the door in their brown overalls which had a big yellow patch on the back. As you can imagine, being Italians, they would try to flirt with us. We used to give them cups of tea as we felt sorry for them. It was hilarious trying to make conversation with them.

As the men started coming back from the war we were made redundant. We were all very sorry to leave as we really enjoyed our time working on the old branch railway.

When I got married in 1953 we went to Bournemouth for our honeymoon, catching the train from Highbridge to Evercreech and then onto the Pines Express. When leaving Highbridge the S&D staff placed detonators on the line so we certainly started our married life with a bang.

I shall never forget my time on the S&D. I often wonder where the other girls are today. At 72, it is nice to have memories of when you were young.

1943

Gordon Hatcher – Passed Fireman

One fright I had which ended up being funny was when I was a young fireman in the 1950s, firing to a grand old driver, Charlie Guy. We were on night banking duties which meant going light engine from Templecombe to Evercreech Junction, then banking night freight trains over the Mendip hills as far as Binegar. This particular evening we were on a 3F Bulldog 0–6–0 engine; having booked on duty at 8.45pm. On the front of this train we had a class 7F engine pulling 66 empty mineral wagons and a guards brake van. All these trains were loose coupled and we were really slogging into it in the Prestleigh Viaduct area. It was a cold winter's night and we were only doing about 10mph. Charlie was on the regulator and I was shovelling for all I was worth. Suddenly against the background of the engine's noise I heard this very loud voice shout out "oy, oy", coming from outside the cab. Charlie nearly had a heart attack and I looked up frightened out of my skin. There was our guard, Larry Maggs, with a big grin on his face standing just outside the cab. What a fright! The Bath guard had come out onto the veranda of his van, stepped across the buffers and walked along the side of the engine and held on to the outside of our cab. I have laughed about this since but I can tell you I didn't at the time.

Gordon Hatcher at Wincanton having a break on the shunting turn. (B.Davis)

When I sit down and think back 40 years about my time on the Somerset & Dorset Railway, it nearly brings tears to my eyes. They were the happiest days of my working life and it was always a pleasure to go to work. It did not matter what time of the day or night you had to book on, we were contented with what we had, a good wife, family, a home and a job that you enjoyed doing; what a difference to latter years. The characters on the S&D will never be replaced, people like Johnny Walker, my father Art Hatcher, Charlie Vaughan and Pip Chant the boilerwasher at Templecombe shed. Wherever you went you always knew someone just like a big family. If I had the chance again I would still do the same. I think the men who worked on the steam engines were a crowd of their own and I was pleased to be involved with them. If only we could turn the clock back to those happy days.

1945

Mark Lambert – Station Foreman

An evening goods train used to come from Highbridge to Evercreech Junction in the 1950s, arriving about 7.00pm, to pick up fitted vans containing powdered milk from Bason Bridge. One particular evening the train was straining up Pylle bank and the driver decided that he could not take the whole train up the bank. To comply with the regulations, he parted the train, securing the rear portion, then took the forward portion into Evercreech sidings. Unfortunately the rear section that was left at Pylle became divided and started to run away under its own power, back through Pylle station, passing Stean Bow crossing. The signalman at West Pennard became aware of this runaway goods train with no engine and switched the train into his sidings. This caused a number of derailments and several fitted vans were completely broken open, throwing their contents of powdered milk over the field behind the down siding of West Pennard station, which was almost opposite the signalbox. I remember this incident well as railway police were on guard there for several days to stop any pilfering. I am sure the station staff did not go short of milk for their tea and I'm told the station cats were licking their lips for many a day.

I recall a story at Elbow Corner crossing near Pylle about a relief crossing keeper in the 1950s. The morning freight from Highbridge crossed over with the 11.05am from Evercreech to Highbridge. At Glastonbury the train turned back, arriving at the crossing at about 12.45pm which was a little earlier than usual. The engine crew whistled to the keeper at Elbow Corner crossing to open the gates. Nothing happened so they whistled again. When the crossing keeper came out of his cottage, he looked at his pocket watch and then shouted out: "You're not due yet, so I'm not opening the crossing gates to let you through." Needless to say a quiet word to the relief crossing keeper from Bill Newman, the Evercreech Junction stationmaster, saved a visit from the district inspector.

Elbow Corner crossing. Note the water cans by the side of the house – there was no running water – and the obligatory warning and trespass signs painted in the reverse to the usual style. (E.Rimmer)

1946

Roy Miles – Guard

My working life on the S&D started as an engine cleaner at Templecombe in 1946. After a time I moved on to become a porter at Blandford Forum, which I really enjoyed. My final and most exciting position was as a guard at Templecombe. I had 20 years of marvellous memories and friendships which I still have to this day. The poem on the following page expresses my personal feelings of my life on the Serene and Delightful.

A Railwayman on the Old S&D

I started in a junior porter's job,
The pay .. well 'twas just a few bob,
But, who cares, to work with good mates
Is better than having a job that one hates.
I'd help load the parcels to go to the town,
Then I'd brush the platforms, the Up and the Down.
When a train arrived, "It's Blandford", I shout,
To make sure the passengers knew where to get out.
Cor this, I thought, is the life for me,
A railwayman on the Old S&D.

These to me were marvellous times,
Steam hauled trains, 'specially the Pines.
This left Blandford at 20 past 10,
Getting to Manchester .. Lord knows when!
Oh! I loved to see this express,
Its coaches maroon and marked L.M.S.
The driver and fireman, with their engine so fine,
Ensured that you got there safely .. on time!
The guard on this train he looked so grand,
With a nice shiny whistle and green flag in his hand.
Then I thought, Ah! that's just right for me,
A passenger Guard on the Old S&D.

There was plenty of rules that had to be learnt,
And a lot of midnight oil was burnt;
But it was worth writing tidy and neat,
When applying for jobs on the vacancy sheet.
They wanted Shunters, Foremen, Lampmen and more,
But I got my job at Templecombe Lower.
In a uniform hat, with a bright golden band,
A shiny new whistle and green flag in my hand,
I was now as proud as could be –
A passenger Guard on the Old S&D.

This Railway had its up and downs –
Going through villages, hamlets and towns.
The farmers in fields at the side of the line,
At the passing of trains, would know the right time.
People going shopping to Bournemouth or Poole,
Others to work and children to school.
Holidaymakers coming South to the sea –
Hoping to get there in time for their tea.
All this meant a lot to we,
Us Railwaymen on the Old S&D.

But, now it seems 'tis only a dream,
Was there really a bridge crossing that stream?
Trees and bushes replace the lines,
And no more will I work the Northbound Pines.
I've long since lost my uniform grand
And have no more use for that flag in my hand.
But, there's one thing they can't take from me –
That's the memories of my friends on the Old S&D.

Roy Miles gives the right of way at Stalbridge in the 1950s. (P.Hatcher)

1947

Dave Boston – Signalman

I started work on the railway on 31st March 1947 in the parcel office at Bristol Temple Meads as a van guard on a horse-drawn cart. After a period of time I transferred to portering duties at St Anne's Park station. Whilst travelling to and from work I met many signalmen and became very interested in this type of work. I applied for Twerton Tunnel signalbox (in Bath) and was accepted for the job. My signalling work took me to various boxes, my favourite being Bath Junction where I spent three happy years on the S&D.

Going back to Twerton (I know it's not S&D territory but I think it is funny enough to whet the appetite). There was an old Elsan toilet next to the signalbox which consisted of an iron frame shaped like a sentry box, covered with corrugated iron sheets. It was not fixed to the ground in any way, and was very rusty and ramshackled; inside was the Elsan bucket. Now one day it happened that Bert Fortune, the ganger, and his men were working close to the box, when the signalman was seen to enter the toilet with his morning newspaper in hand. The members of the gang waited long enough for him to settle down. Now here I must explain that the box and toilet was situated on a slight bank from which the main A4 road could be clearly seen across the sports field behind the box. About four members of the gang crept over to the toilet with one man on each corner. They swiftly lifted the whole toilet clear of the poor old signalman who was sat there with shirt tail in hand in full view of the busy A4. There he sat shouting and cursing the gang until they replaced it. They then made a rapid departure.

One day the same signalman was about to have his breakfast in the box when to his horror he found his wife had forgotten to put his usual egg in his lunchbox. After giving it some thought he decided to take an egg from the henhouse belonging to Albert Perkins, the Stothert and Pitt groundsman. The henhouse was about 50 yards from the box so he climbed through the fence, keeping a sharp eye on Albert's bungalow, and crawled on all fours through the long grass until he reached the nesting boxes. He then slipped his hand into the box and carefully removed an egg, put it in his pocket and made his way back to the fence. He went into the signalbox feeling very proud of himself until he removed the egg from his pocket and found that he had taken the china egg for broody hens.

When I was at Bath Junction in 1961 I must have been the first signalman to put a diesel on S&D metals by mistake. It was the 10.15pm to York parcel train. I relieved Bob Drew, the 2.00pm–10.00pm signalman. Whilst we were talking after the handover, I had the call attention signal from Bath Green Park box (Charlie Perkins) who then sent me what I took to be 1–3 which I understood was the passenger train for the S&D preceding the York parcels, which was not unusual. Charlie never questioned my reply so I got the road from Midford, withdrew the tablet, took it out and fixed it in the catcher, and then set the road and signals for that line. Bob Drew was still in the box standing by the frame chatting, when I received the train entering section signal from Charlie. I answered the signal and sat down again. About a minute later Bob looked out of the window and shouted: "Bloody hell! Thats not the passenger, it's the parcels." By the time I had got to the frame it was too late, the parcels, headed by the diesel, shot up the S&D line. Brakes screeching and sparks flying, it ground to a halt up on the road bridge. Bob ran out to see the driver whilst I phoned Charlie and got permission for the train to set back. On his way back the driver stopped and told me that he was too busy watching the Weston signalbox red home signal to notice that the green one was for the S&D. He said it frightened him to death because when he shot off wrong road to the left he thought for a moment that he had come off the road. Anyway all was squared up in S&D fashion amongst ourselves and nothing more was ever heard about it.

In 1962 I was on the late shift, 2.00–10.00pm, when a gentleman turned up opposite the signalbox with a rather expensive movie camera. He came up the stairs and entered the box in order to introduce himself. It just happened to be the well-known S&D photographer, Ivo Peters. He filmed me coming out of the box with the tablet and fixing it into the automatic catcher. This shot can now be seen on his video *Bath to Masbury*.

I well remember the bad winter of 1962/3. I was working the late shift if I remember correctly. I think Bert Henman, the district inspector, was visiting

Bath Junction signalbox with Bath Gas Works gasholders in the background. (I.Patrick)

the box when it started to snow quite hard. Bert seemed to think it would just be a quick shower. When he could see that it did not look like stopping he urgently made his way down to his office. The snow kept coming down until it started creeping over the top of the rails and I had to send for the track gang to come out and clear the points. I tried to clear them myself but it was hopeless. When they arrived they worked very hard clearing away the snow from the points. These men were to stay working at the box for the next three months (this was the worst winter in S&D history). The signalbox stayed open continuously throughout this period. The S&D line was blocked by a huge snowdrift at Masbury, two trains were buried in the snow and the train crews had to abandon them.

It was decided to send a snow plough over the S&D to clear the line. When the engine turned up I could not help but laugh as they had sent a Jinty with just a small plough on the front which was only just below the buffer beam. It went out but was found to be quite useless, so a Mogul tender engine was sent to Bath. This had a huge plough, the width of the engine, and went right up to the chimney. I remember when Ron Moore, the permanent way inspector, told me of his experience on the footplate that day. The driver, as far as I know, was Ken Norris. There was also a locomotive inspector on board. Ron said that when the inspector arrived at this mountain of snow which was blocking the cutting, he asked Ken to back the engine up and then give her all he could. They hit the wall of snow and there was an almighty shudder. He thought the engine was coming off the road and snow went everywhere. Ron said he'd never experienced anything like it in his life.

January 1963. From left to right, Jack Walbridge, Bert Clarke and Joe Easterbrook wait for a towing chain to haul 47557 out of a snowdrift north of Winsor Hill. (J.Stamp)

This action was continued until they hammered their way through.

The cold weather went on and on; there was still snow in April. It did have one good point, though. When I was working the night shift the members of the gang used to spend a lot of time in the box, and this was nice because we used to have a chat and tell yarns whilst drinking hot tea by a nice coal fire. We all got to know each other much better.

Alan Larcombe was a porter at Bath Green Park station and a good friend of mine. He would often take over the duties of lampman. One day I spotted Alan coming up the track towards the box. I knew that he was doing the lampman's job so I nipped downstairs and without him seeing me I picked up two handfuls of ballast and put them down on the veranda on top of the signalbox stairs. When Alan arrived at the lamp room which was close to the box he shouted his greetings which I acknowledged; he then went into the lamp room which was made of corrugated iron and proceeded to fill the lamps and trim the wicks, leaving one lamp burning to light the other lamps with. The lamp room door was wide open so that when I crept out onto the veranda I could see him working away. I picked up the ballast and dropped the lot on the roof. For a second Alan froze and then he blew out the lamp and came out like a rocket. It was only when he saw me laughing my head off that he realized what had happened, and for a few minutes the air was blue, but he took it all in good fun. When we were both on nights he often came up to see me on his motor scooter which he left at the bottom of the bank. One night in particular he came up after the last passenger train. We had our usual chat and a cup of tea, now this would be around midnight. He had to be back at the station by about 1.45am to prepare the 2.40am train. After a while Alan decided to have a sleep so he stretched out along the lever frame which is raised. He fell into a deep sleep and somehow he fell off the frame. I swear he never woke up but crawled back onto the frame without opening his eyes and was gone again. Because it was quiet at this time of night and as Alan was asleep I thought I would have a good read. Sad to say I forgot about the time so when I did look up at the clock I realized that Alan should now be down at the station; it was about 1.50am. I shouted at him to wake up but he never moved, he was out cold. I shook him and shouted at him but I could not wake him up. I had never known anything like it and I wondered what the hell I could do to awaken him. Then I had an idea, my whistle, so I got it out of my locker and blew it as hard as I could. He opened his eyes, stood up, walked out of the box and down the path, got on his scooter and away he went; he never said a word.

Another incident I remember involved a collision at Bath Green Park station in 1962 when a parcel train was put into the platform for loading and then withdrawn. Normally the foreman in charge in such a case would advise the signalman if any vans or wagons were to be left in the platform. This was necessary because there were no track circuits and the signalman could not see right into the station. On this particular occasion the parcel train was withdrawn and because the foreman did not inform my mate Charlie Perkins of any vans having been left in the platform, he assumed that it was clear and took the passenger train which was offered to him. I pulled off all my signals and so did he, unaware that there was an obstruction. The station was situated around a left-hand bend so it was not until the train was almost entering the station that the driver could see the platform. In this instance the poor driver never had a chance. He applied full emergency brakes but it was too late and the train hit the vans, causing quite a lot of damage to the end of the platform. Some of the men who were working in the vans were injured, though none very seriously, but I do remember a woman porter was hurt the most. I had to attend the inquiry and poor Charlie took all of the blame. It really had nothing to do with Charlie; it was fully the foreman's fault, as he should have informed the signalman.

I enjoyed my days at Bath and had some good mates like signalmen Bob Drew, Ernie Cross, George Smart, Len Ryan and Ivor Patrick. Whenever Ivor was at Midford box we used to send each other silly poems in the tablet pouch – all good fun.

1947

Cliff Smith – Fireman

I started as a cleaner at Bath Green Park in August 1947. A lot of the men I worked with started on the S&D after they were demobbed from the services. For a time I was in the same gang as John Spencer, an ex-sailor who lived not far from the shed. When we were on the afternoon turn he told me to go to his flat just after 8.00pm and his wife would give us some bread pudding. This happened every Wednesday. The pudding was still hot and we shared it with the other members of the gang who were Frank Tutton, Jim Towels, Jim Cantello, George Austin and Bill Thornton.

When I became a fireman we used to take out the 5.00pm market train from Bath to Evercreech. This train was booked to shunt at various stations to pick up cattle that had been bought at market. After carrying out the shunting we turned the locomotive at Evercreech ready to work to Bath following the last up passenger. We had quite a long time at Evercreech so we often went to the *Railway Hotel* to eat our supper with a glass of cider. I remember one driver on this turn, Jim Machin, who came from the North of England. We were in the pub having our supper when in came a farmer who was well known to the landlord. The farmer had a cow which was due to calf. "How's the calf?" asked the landlord.

From left to right, Roy Williams, Cliff Smith and Len Pond pose happily in the cab of Stanier class 5, No 45056, in 1948. (C.Smith collection)

"All right," answered the farmer, "but it came at 3 o'clock this morning and I only had the village lantern to see by." My mate asked me what the village lantern was and I had to explain to him that it was the moon; he had never heard it called that before.

I remember firing the 4.15pm Templecombe to Bath in the late 1950s. The coal on the tender was picked up from a stack which had been down for years and the coal was dead. Anyway we got to Masbury with a struggle and when we stopped we did not have enough steam to get the brakes off. I looked back to let the guard know we would be about five minutes to get going again. While looking back I noticed in the front coach there was a girl from Sunnyhill School, Bruton, and she called out: "Hurry up, I've got to get home to change as I have to see my boyfriend tonight." After sweating and doing my best, that was all I wanted. She really thought that it was my fault that we had no steam.

I left Bath Green Park in 1962 as I could see the S&D coming to an end and I transferred to Bristol. While working over the S&D, although it was hard work, it seemed more enjoyable than on the Western. I recall one Christmas Eve I was firing the 4.37pm stopper to Templecombe and coming back on the last up to Bath. This train left Templecombe at 8.51pm. My driver,

Sid Cater, and myself went to *The Royal Hotel* for a glass of lemonade with our supper. Outside the pub the local choir turned up, singing beautiful carols. I could have stayed there all night. These sort of things don't happen any more.

After all these years I still have close contact with my former Bath mates, Ron Gray, Arthur Turner, Mike Ryall, George Tucker and Jack Cook. A glass of cider and a chat about the old days is something I look forward to.

1949

Bill Silk – Fireman

My S&D career started in October 1949 as a cleaner at Templecombe, my wages were 39/6 per week. I had to cycle five miles to get there but that was something that everyone did in those days including the senior railwaymen who were in their sixties. They cycled in all sorts of weather and at all hours which of course included the early turn and on many occasions they were soaked through before they started work.

As cleaners, there were times when you were put on labouring duties. We did not mind this as we got the going rate which was £4 12/6 per week. We started at 6.00am and part of the job was coaling engines. We would fill up approximately nine engine tenders before breakfast which was at 8.00am. Some of those tenders could take 12 tubs of coal and there was 7cwt in each coaling tub. We would wind up what we called the mangle. This was a crane operated by two men on a platform about 15 feet off the ground. They would wind a cog wheel, one on each side of the crane. There was a double jib that swung out, one tub going down and one coming up. They swung the loaded one into the tender and I recall that the old 3F Bulldog engines for the night banker used to take 12 to 14 tubs of coal.

Another job we used to do was to call up the drivers in the early morning around Templecombe. We used to do this only on a Sunday as Percy Gedge did the job all the rest of the week. You would get a slip from the chargehand with the name and address of the railwayman you had to knock up for duty. Percy was renowned for going into the messroom and washing all the cups in a bucket. Unfortunately it was the same bucket that he had put paraffin in for cleaning various items.

After a period of time I became a passed cleaner which allowed you to carry out firing turns. Initially they put you on shunting duties.

I remember my first trip to Bath with Ben Dyer. It was on a night special (ammunition). We got into Bath in pitch darkness except for a few flickering gas lamps. It was rather eerie and a bit frightening for a young lad especially with ammunition behind you but Ben looked after me like a father and there were no problems. Later when working the summer specials from Bournemouth to Bath, I had another experience. My first driver on the specials was Bill Bailey, a smashing bloke. I had only fired on a small engine with a three coach set behind. One day I was with Bill and we had a big LMS Black 5 with 12 coaches on. Bill said to me: "Fill her up, Billy." I filled the firebox up like I did at Templecombe. Bill looked at me and said: "Give me the shovel, I'll show you how to fill her up properly." He started shovelling and I thought he was going to empty the tender, I couldn't believe it. Bill was like a human dynamo. As we left Bournemouth I could see why he had filled her up; there was such a pull on the firebox as it was all uphill. That taught me an early lesson in future firing turns when working with the Bournemouth drivers. There were some superb drivers at Branksome. Donald Beale is the best known name but there were others that came in the same category like Arthur Clist. He was a real gem of a man and always gave you plenty of encouragement and help. Other drivers there included Alec Bolwell, John Flynn, Bert Freakley, Eric Elford and Bert Brewer.

Getting onto Bath loco on a hot summer Saturday was unbelievable and trying to get coal under the coal stage was nearly impossible. There were engines queueing everywhere and shunting around. It was a fight for survival, especially in hot smoky humid conditions.

I recall my first turn to Bridgwater with Harry Jeans. It was just before the closure of the line and it was a sad sight coming into the rundown station where once there had been a hive of activity and where many Bridgwater railwaymen had worked, like Will Locke, Fred Lester, and father and son Gilbert and Dennis Ashill.

Gilbert Ashill stands proudly by S&D lorry No 4692 at Bridgwater in the 1920s. The Bath-registered vehicle is possibly a Karrier model K. Note the large pneumatic tyres (single at the rear), oil lamps, bulb horn and open cab. The load of boxes and crates would never be seen today. (D.Ashill collection)

After some time I became a fireman at Templecombe. There were many grades of railwaymen there who taught you a thing or two and you became good mates with them. There were two steamraisers, Walt Webb and George Merchant, the boilersmith was Joe Dyer, Ben Dyer's father. He was a great big stout man who loved his tea. We often used to say that after drinking so much tea and getting in a quite warm firebox he would swell up and wouldn't be able to get out. He was a tough fellow and carried on with this hard job well into his sixties. The drivers there were a great bunch to work with, people like Ray Stokes, Bert Jones, Trevor Netley, Ben Dyer, Lou Long and Fritz Lawrence who was the local unofficial bookmaker for everybody.

In those days there was a dedication to the job, giving a service to the public. The passenger was the most important person and to be late with the train was a crime. There was a stigma attached to you if you lost a minute and didn't get there on time.

The guard played a major part in the running of the train especially goods trains. I rode spare many times in the goods guards van when going to Bournemouth and I used to marvel at their expertise with the handbrake. In some places on the Dorset it was quite undulating. On a 55-wagon loose-coupling goods train part of it could be going uphill, part downhill and part on the level. The guard, in conjunction with the driver, would keep those couplings tight. Failure to do this could result in the snatching of the couplings which could cause a breakage. I remember Art Hatcher telling me of a time when driver Jimmy Good and himself were coming over Corfe Mullen bank with the night Poole goods. They started to pull away towards Bailey Gate (the goods vans had side lights on and this enabled the footplate crew to look back to make sure the van was coming). On this occasion Art looked back towards the van and said to Jimmy, "he's not coming". They immediately stopped the train and moved back down the line until they found the van. They had snatched a wagon clean in half, leaving the guards van behind the now depleted wagon.

Fireman Art Hatcher (left) and driver Jimmy Good pictured on Weymouth sands having brought a Sunday School excursion from Templecombe in the 1920s. Note Art's bow tie. (G.Hatcher collection)

Much has been said about trains from Bath getting stuck in the snowdrifts on the Mendips in 1963 and how crews went to their aid from Bath. I was a fireman on a train coming from Templecombe on a rescue mission to recover the stranded engine and vans of the down mail from Bath. I was on the front engine which was a Tanky with a snow plough and my driver was Jack Hix. Behind us on a Standard class 4 engine was driver Les Cuss and fireman Clive Burden. The third engine was also a Standard 4 with driver Lou Long and fireman Alan Hix. All three engines set off coupled together with Alec Stowe, the Evercreech Junction stationmaster, on board. We arrived at the big snowdrifts at Winsor Hill tunnel and made our way towards Masbury. It was unbelievable; the snow was solid across the cutting. We were charging into the drifts to try and shift them. With all three regulators open you can imagine

From left to right, Lou Long, Bill Silk, Alan Hix and Clive Burden stand in front of snowbound locomotives near Masbury in January 1963. (B.Silk collection)

the power and force that was involved. We came to a standstill about 150 yards from where the Bath engine was. Where we had hit the snow trying to clear the line there were enormous boulders of snow as big as your dining room by the side of the track. Eventually after several attempts to move the drift we saw the top of the chimney of the mail train. We walked forward to examine what we could do. The engine and vehicles were completely buried. We decided to take our three engines back to a certain point, then to charge into the drift, making sure there was a distance from us and the mail train. It was agreed by the three drivers that they would shut their regulators off at a certain telegraph pole. Unfortunately one of the drivers did not understand the instructions and did not shut off his regulator at the same time as the other two. The consequences were that we did not slow down as quickly as we hoped. We hit the mail train with a wallop, my driver Jack Hix was knocked to the floor and cut his face, the stationmaster fell on top of him and I was flung against the firebox front and twisted my shoulder. Fortunately nobody was seriously hurt. We got off the footplate to examine the damage but we still couldn't see much because of the snow. We certainly moved the train. When we got on the mail train engine we could see all the gauge glasses were broken. This was caused by all the fire irons and coal shooting off the tender and coming into the cab. We had also smashed our snow plough which was now useless. We decided we would couple up and pull the engine and the ten vans back to Shepton Mallet so we hooked up and went to pull out. After a few seconds of pulling we realized this was an impossible task and on closer examination of the train we found that when we had hit the engine and vans they had gone straight up into the air. They couldn't go backwards because the snow was solid. Unfortunately they did not come back down on the track, they were all derailed. What a mess! We had to leave them there and go back to Shepton Mallet to dump the snow plough. The breakdown gang then came out from Bristol by road. They had to come down in treacherous conditions to try and get the wagons back on the rails and I gather it took them three days to do this.

Another thing about that winter I remember was that we had a thermometer on the side of the foreman's office in Templecombe Lower yard.

I can remember all that winter right through until late March the thermometer never rose above 19 degrees fahrenheit, night and day. Now that is cold.

A few years ago the *Western Daily Press* ran features about passengers' experiences on the S&D. Reading one day about a lady explaining about the time she was late for a train, I realized she was talking about myself and my driver. That night my driver, Ray Stokes, and myself came up from Bournemouth on the 6.40 up. That train connected with the last up train to London at Templecombe so it was important you were on time. I remember we got to Blandford and the porter came up to us and said: "There is a woman with two young children who have missed the train at Bournemouth. The stationmaster has got a taxi for her to bring her to Blandford." We waited and waited for her and it seemed ages before the taxi arrived but eventually it did and she scrambled onto the train with her children. We had a good Standard class 4 engine. I said to Ray: "Well, we will be late for this connection." He replied: "Don't worry we'll make it." Talk about give it the gun, by the time we had got to the top of the little bank out of Blandford I reckon we were doing 70mph. We did Blandford to Templecombe, stopping at all the stations, in under 20 minutes, which was unbelievable, and arrived in time for the lady to catch her connection. In the letter the lady wrote to the paper she said how wonderful the footplate crew and the staff at Bournemouth and Blandford had been.

Travelling along fairly fast on a railway engine you would occasionally get areas under one of the sleepers that needed packing. When you went over these loose sleepers the engine would drop and nearly knock you over on the footplate. The way they used to detect these bad areas in my early days was from an observation coach, on each side of which they had a cut-away section on the floor with a bowl of whitewash hung down. As the train went along, every time the wheel dropped on a bad piece of sleeper it would slurp the whitewash out. The whitewash would indicate to the permanent way men when they came along that this was a bad one that needed packing.

I qualified as a driver with a lot of help from one of the senior drivers, Pat Evans. I remember the rule book had 250 rules in it and you certainly needed help with that. Equally important was your knowledge of the working parts of the engine. You were questioned quite extensively by the inspector passing you out. My first trip on my own was with fireman Cliff Day. We took the 11.40 from Bournemouth to Bath, taking over at No 2 signalbox at Templecombe. I had many driving trips with many memories but that is another story.

1949

Eric Miles – Signalman

I returned home in 1948 after spending five years in the army. I went back to work on the farm where I had previously worked. I had been happy there. My brother Roy was working on the S&D at Blandford.

Memories of my grandfather's stories about his days as a signalman at Clapham Junction fired my enthusiasm to become a railwayman. On my day off I cycled the 15 miles to Blandford station (a journey that I was to get to know very well). On arrival at the station I asked to see the stationmaster, Mr Albert Powis, who was to give me plenty of help and encouragement later on in my railway life. I asked him if there were any vacancies. "Not at present but I will take your name," he replied. On telling him my name he said: "Funny that, I have just lost a man with the same name to the Air Force [National Service]." I replied: "That was my brother" and he immediately said: "Let's see what we can do for you, your brother Roy gave us good service." Within the week I had a post as temporary holiday relief porter. It was goodbye to farming and the start of my 25-year life on the railway. On that 15-mile bike ride to Blandford to start my job I wondered if I had done the right thing. I am pleased to say that I never looked back and was proud to work on the S&D.

I was introduced to all the staff and taken under the wing of a grand old porter called Charlie Preston who had a very dry sense of humour. His first words to me were: "If thee be like your brother thee won't be much bother, right this is lamp morning." So off we went in the direction of a tin shed, which was the lamp house. We picked up a collection of lamps and carried them in the direction of the tallest signal. On arrival at the signal Charlie said: "Well, young 'un, aloft you go." I looked up, petrified, took a deep breath, and started my journey upwards, lamp in hand and cotton waste in my pocket, eyes firmly fixed at the top. The signal was swaying at every step. I reached the top, got onto the small wooden platform, changed the lamp, cleaned the lens, and brought the old lamp down to the ground to take away and clean.

A couple of days later the Blandford signalman invited me up for a cup of tea. The signalbox was another world and I was struck how clean it was, everything polished and spotless. The signalman asked me if I was interested in becoming a signalman as there was a temporary vacancy in Blandford box. I told him that I really was so I made out the necessary application forms and sent them off to Bath. A week or two later I was accepted and received notification to start at Blandford box with tutor signalman Ken Eveleigh. After about six weeks I was called to Bath to see the district inspector for a test on rules and regulations. I must have impressed him as he said he would be down to Blandford to observe me working the box. Ken, who had given me a lot of help, was pleased as it allowed him to leave for temporary relief signalman which he had applied for. One side of Blandford box was single-line operated with electric tokens to Shillingstone, the other side was double-line block to Bailey Gate. The great day arrived when I took over Blandford box on my own; the first thing was to send 5/5/5 bells to Shillingstone (opening of the box). I stayed at Blandford for three months as the post was temporary. Blandford had an army camp and there were a lot of troops coming and going (National Service lads). On Thursdays two trains would arrive in the morning full of lads in their civvies and two trains in the evening, one going north and the other one to London, taking trained soldiers to their new camps.

I remember on one occasion a train pulled in one evening full of lads who had been on leave. I saw two of them hanging back so I leaned out of the box and said: "You two got tickets?" Their answer was: "Well, no, we haven't." As I had been a soldier for five years I felt sorry for them, and pointed: "Quick, down that path into the street." Unfortunately, unbeknown to me, at the end of the path were two redcaps. My good turn had gone wrong.

Standard class 4, No 75073, enters Blandford station in 1965 with a Bath train consisting of a GUV van and three Bulleid coaches. Note the high signalbox. (D.Walden)

I worked at many signalboxes on the S&D. I recall working as a relief signalman at Burnham-on-Sea signalbox. One particular day I had a raging toothache. Charlie King, one of the old time S&D drivers, suggested I go and see his dentist who was a friend of his in Burnham and get it sorted. I did not want to leave my duties so I stayed until my turn had finished then walked up the road to the dentist and saw the receptionist who said they could not see me for three days. I happened to mention I was a friend of Charlie King; the receptionist spoke to the dentist who came out of his room and offered to pull the tooth out there and then. I sat in the dentist's chair and he mentioned to me that he was an S&D railway enthusiast. He never stopped talking about the railway. I opened my mouth and he started working on my tooth which he extracted. Unfortunately he had been so interested in the S&D that he pulled out the wrong tooth, alas a perfectly good one. Realizing his mistake he apologized and pulled out the offending tooth. It was such a relief that I didn't complain.

As a signalman the most important thing to check after a thunderstorm was that the phones worked between signalboxes and crossings. When I was at Glastonbury signalbox we had a really bad storm and the phone lines went dead. That evening a young lady arrived drenched at the signalbox to tell me that she was the crossing keeper at Cemetery Lane and did I know that the telephone line was down. After her initial visit we became very friendly and later we married. We had over 30 years of happy marriage but unfortunately Joyce passed away in 1987. I must say what a wonderful job these lady crossing keepers did, they worked long hours and seldom complained. They were a very important part of the railway.

Living at Cemetery Lane crossing with Joyce was very idyllic and I thoroughly enjoyed it. Unfortunately the cottage has been pulled down to make way for the new Glastonbury by-pass, another part of the S&D link

4F, No 44557, enters Glastonbury station with two GWR coaches in tow, bound for Evercreech Junction, in June 1959. (R.E.Toop)

destroyed. We lived in the cottage long enough to see the line between Evercreech Junction and Highbridge close. The saddest time was when the line was lifted.

In the early days at Glastonbury signalbox I recall the floods that came after periods of heavy rain. Looking out of the box it was like an inland sea with trees and the tops of hedges showing above the water.

My father-in-law, Sam Bailey, was a lorry driver/goods porter at Glastonbury station. One day a farmer arrived at the station asking for the stationmaster. Sam pointed him in the right direction and said: "By the way he's very deaf, don't forget to shout." The farmer arrived at the stationmaster's office and nearly knocked the door down. The door opened and the farmer walked in. After their conversation the stationmaster said to the farmer: "Yes, we can do some business but in future please don't shout, I'm not deaf, you know."

Colleagues that I worked with at Glastonbury were shunter Ken Atkins, district relief porter Percy Parsons, porters Ted Cook, Percy Bishop, Ern Pike and foreman Hugh Durston.

Oh to be in a Somerset & Dorset signalbox again.

1949

Paul Fry – Booking Clerk

My father Bob was a great influence in me joining the S&D. He worked at Wells and we lived in the station house there. I recall one humorous story he told me. He had an allotment next to the railway at Wells where he grew many vegetables and one year he had a lovely crop of rhubarb. One Friday afternoon a Western goods train passed by and the rhubarb went with it; the footplate crew did not realize it was Bob's allotment. Now my father had a good idea who these Western lads were and he waited until the time was right to get his own back on them. He did not have to wait too long. He was a guard on a freight train with a very heavy load and the two culprits were the driver and fireman up front. When they got to Shepton Mallet where the bank was 1 in 46 he waited until they were just at the bottom of the gradient then quietly screwed down the brakes on the goods van at the back, bit by bit and carefully. Slower and slower they went until they almost stopped. Then he let the brake off and they slowly got underway again. When they had picked up a bit, down the brake went again. The driver could not make it out and the fireman began to sweat, shovelling more and more coal into the hungry firebox, trying to make more steam. The driver whistled to my father but he pretended that all was well at the back, and waved the green flag at them. When they got to Shepton Mallet the fireman was almost exhausted and the driver was as red as a beetroot. Father slowly walked up to the engine and straight-faced and in front of others enquired whether they knew how to drive and fire an engine, as he had never had such a poor trip, and if this was a passenger train they would have got a lost time ticket. He felt the sweating, confusion and embarrassment he had caused was revenge enough and went smiling on his way. Father had a spell as a shunter and acting guard at both the Evercreech stations in the 1930s. He was renowned for having his own personal frying pan from which he would enjoy his breakfast in the shunters' cabin at Evercreech Junction with one of his great friends Jack Harvey.

Bob Fry's great friend, Jack Harvey, head shunter at Evercreech Junction, in 1947. (P.Parsons)

When he left the Junction the other shunters gave him some poetry that they had compiled called *Departure of Fry*.

> All our shunters got the fly,
> Because they lost their little Fry.
> The ozone of his bit of bacon
> Is present now at another station.
> He wasn't a bad old sort, old Bob,
> Was also one who knew his job,
> Especially if down branch came in
> He would do an awful grin.
> When acting guard up at the New
> The 'Binegar' he loved to see run through
> Because old Harvey then would sweat,
> Especially when 'twas very wet.
> Good old Fry, they all gone dry
> Since you have left this station
> And the frypan has become
> A tool of stagnation.
> They didn't give you half your rights
> Whilst shunting at this Junction.
> But poor old Harvey's got the hump
> Now he can't watch you munching.
> Another pan he'll have to buy
> Because of rafty bacon.
> He's going to get it and will charge
> The purchase to your station.
> So now old chum just do your best
> And put it well across 'em
> If they should send a wagon on
> That should be taken off 'em.
> Poor old Jack is going to cry
> 'Cos he's lost his old pal Fry,
> So send him in a bit of 'baccy
> That will make the old bloke happy.

I spent some time in the 1950s as a booking clerk at West Pennard. Our stationmaster was Reg Jeans, a fine railwayman and an excellent chap to work with. He took a pride in his appearance as befitted the stationmaster and always wore a clean white collar to work. One Monday morning Reg was walking around the station and the Highbridge to Evercreech freight had just arrived with a class 4 loco in charge. It stopped with the cab right under the road bridge to the east end of the station. Reg was just walking past under the bridge when the Ross pop valves opened up with a roar, the steam hitting the underside of the bridge and bringing down a deluge of black sooty hot water. Reg appeared in the office a few minutes later covered with soot and his pure white shirt and collar blackened. Not much upset Reg but this did and he had to go off home to change. Knowing how he felt, nothing was said till some time after.

Two passengers wait on West Pennard down platform in 1964. How peaceful it all seems. (C.Caddy)

There was a Ministry of Food buffer depot built during the war near the station with its own siding. It was used to store foodstuffs such as flour, sugar, tea and tinned milk, and we seldom went short of these whilst I was at the station. At one time the store was overrun with vermin and the Ministry decided that it should be cleared. All the doors were sealed except one which was left wide open. High planks were laid down from this door converging like a trap. I heard that gas was introduced into the building at the opposite end to the trap and as it went through the store the vermin came scrambling out of the open door only to meet their death at the hands of a team of workers each armed with a stout stick with which they were quickly despatched. It was carried out this way so that no dead vermin bodies were left inside or so I was told.

The Ministry used to hire all sorts of people to do the loading and unloading. There was one man who I think had been a weight-lifter as he often did his party trick of walking up a loading ramp with a one-cwt bag under each arm. He would challenge anyone else to do the same.

There was another challenge put out by the local coal merchant, George Carey, who was the agent for John Snow & Company and used the yard at Pennard as his base. He was a smallish man but very strong and with the knack of lifting, obtained from years of experience. The challenge was to throw a 56-lb metal scale weight right over the top of a railway box van. Many tried and many failed and the coalman took the money. One day however the tables were turned on him after quite a few cups of scrumpy taken at lunchtime in the *Railway Inn*. When he was rather unsteady on his pins he was bet quite a considerable sum that he could not carry a one-cwt sack of coal along the edge of an eight-foot crossing timber. The timber was to be set up on top of two other timbers and made secure. The top would have been about 2ft 6ins from the ground. The challenge was that he should get up with the sack unaided and walk the length, turn round and walk back. A few more cups were put away and Reg Jeans held the money. The assembled company moved to the goods yard where the timbers were and a full sack of coal was found. To everyone's amazement he managed to get up and walk along the top of the timbers. Unfortunately with many cups of scrumpy under his belt he tried to turn, slipped and fell, injuring his back. He was off work for some time; however, the bet was given to him as compensation for his loss of wages.

The road bridge over the line was askew with a sharp left, then a sharp right. This caused problems for motorists especially when the road was icy. Reg and myself were sat in the office one day when we heard a bang from the direction of the bridge. We did not take too much notice but a few minutes later a very angry army major stormed into the office demanding something be done pretty damn quickly, and who was going to pay the compensation to him. What had happened was that as he was driving his brand new Jaguar from Shepton Mallet to Glastonbury, he had taken the bridge far too fast and had managed to burst both his nearside tyres on the semi-circular stones which projected from the side of the bridge. He was not amused and threatened to sue all and sundry. It did not help when Reg asked if the bridge was moving or stationary. Reg also pointed out that the stones had been there for over 60 years.

As an officer in charge of the City of Wells division of the St John Ambulance and a former S&D booking and goods clerk at Wells, I well remember railways were very keen on their staff being trained in first aid. The Somerset and Dorset joint committee and the Great Western Railway at Wells were no exception. There was a desire by all the railway management to get their staff involved with useful activities, so that team spirit would be developed. The Wells unit came into existence in 1929. The stationmasters of the S&D and the GWR were contacted and a meeting was arranged. Eight staff from all departments of the two companies offered to become involved.

My father Glencoe William Charles Fry (S&D), known as Bob by his workmates, was a founder member, having obtained his certificate in 1921 through the London and South Western Railway Centre of the St John Ambulance Association following an examination taken at Glastonbury. Other S&D railwaymen in the St John Ambulance Association were Bill Wotton who acted as secretary, Victor Salway, Harry Pearce and Ernest Baker. The GWR men were Wilf Coleman, Bill Potter and Wilf Hickman. Every year first aid teams from various S&D stations competed for the St John Ambulance Association shield, a highly prestigious trophy to win. It really was the enthusiasm and dedication of the railway staff that started the Wells division and saw it continue until the railways sadly vanished from the town.

1950

John Holt – Fireman

A few memories come to mind when firing in the 1950s. I was out with a grand old driver, Art Hatcher, on a little Tanky engine and had stopped at Templecombe Upper yard for a spot of lunch. Art got off the engine and went to cut a stick from a nearby hedge. He came back onto the cab and, took this massive bloater out of his lunchbox and skewered it onto the stick. I was

John Holt and driver Den Norris gaze happily from the cab of 3F, No 43216, in 1959. (P.Hatcher)

heaving already. He looked at me and grinned, and put it into the firebox What a smell! The smoke was wafting out of the firebox and after a minute or two I couldn't stand it any longer so when Art was not looking I touched the blower on the engine. Immediately the bloater disappeared off its stick and went straight up the chimney. Art's face dropped as he realized his dinner had gone and he didn't speak to me again for the rest of the day. The next day it had all been forgotten and we had a jolly good laugh about it.

I was firing to driver Ben Dyer one day when we had a trainee on board, learning the ropes. We were taking the Pines Express to Bath and when we reached Midsomer Norton, which is near Norton Hill colliery, Ben winked at me. He turned to the trainee and said: "If you listen carefully and put your head down to the cab floor you will hear the miners picking with their picks." The lad was led down on the cab floor listening out for these miners, turning from one ear to another and screwing his face up trying to hear the noises. He would have been there all day only we couldn't stand it any longer and burst out laughing.

Another time I was with driver Ted Elliot, working the shunting engine at Evercreech Junction. Ted looked into the firebox and said: "Don't put any more coal on for a bit. We haven't got anything to do and we can have a few minutes' shut-eye." So we both made ourselves comfortable in the cab. The next thing we knew it's panic; a train had arrived from Bath and was waiting to be shunted. The yard lights were flashing on and off to gain our attention. Ted shouted out to me: "Quick look in the firebox." The fire was right out; porters and shunters were looking for anything that would burn to re-light the fire and make some steam. Pieces of wood and other items were quickly put into the firebox, I poked around with a long pricker and managed to get it alight. We never went to sleep again in the cab.

Part of our work was connected with the Highbridge branch. We used to work a train from Highbridge to Templecombe called The Highbridge Market. It was quite a heavy and long train and contained mostly coal which had been delivered by boat into Highbridge Wharf. We used to cross a passenger train from Evercreech Junction at Shapwick station. Just a few yards from the station was a public house called *The Griffin Head*, sadly no longer standing. On hot days we used to pop in and quench our thirst with the local brew. One day we were just finishing our drink in the public bar when we heard the passenger train coming down the line. It gave us just enough time to finish our drink and get aboard our engine. It was my job to exchange hand signals with the guard, Hugh

Hugh Berryman in 1958 at Park Lane crossing where he lived with his wife who was the crossing keeper. He gave 39 years service to the S&D. (J.Fisher collection)

Berryman (his daughter is the well-known S&D lady Joan Fisher). As we were pulling out from Shapwick with our long train I kept looking back at the guards van. The sun was quite blinding as it was setting in the sky. I said to my driver, Jack Osborne: "I haven't seen the guard yet." He came over to my side of the engine and had a look. Jack said "I expect he's OK", and off we set. We thought the train seemed extra heavy (unbeknown to us the guards brake was still on) but we managed to keep going. When we were approaching Glastonbury the home signal was red so we got right up to it and then it went to green, but the signalman slowed us down with a red flag from the signalbox so we approached with caution and stopped. The signalman was in quite a panic, he shouted out: "You haven't got a guard, you left him at Shapwick." We were now in real trouble. The signalman seeing the expression on my face said: "Don't worry, someone is bringing him here on a motorbike." Sure enough a motorbike came whizzing round the bend with Hugh hanging on for dear life. Fortunately the Shapwick signalman saw the predicament and drove him there. We were most grateful and bought him a pint at *The Griffin Head* when we went there again. We heard no more about it – good old S&D loyalty.

1950

John Badman – Booking Clerk

My family has been involved with the Somerset & Dorset Railway since 1883, when my mother's father, Edmond Ham, was asked to report to Nathaniel Meech, the Binegar stationmaster, to start his duties as a porter at the station.

He gave 46 years service to the S&D and reached the pinnacle of his career by being made stationmaster at Shapwick and later at Bailey Gate where he retired. He was a stationmaster for 25 years. When he had retired I used to visit him at his railway cottage at Bailey Gate. Being the former stationmaster there, he would take me to the station and introduce me to everybody. There was a nice old porter there called Percy Carter. I would write out labels for the milk wagons from the local milk factory. When the lorry came in with the corn which went to the local mill for grinding, the driver would pick up these old West of England $2^{1}/_{4}$-cwt sacks of corn. He just trundled them up with a sack truck, catching hold and topping them himself; as he said, "all in a day's work".

My mother, Florence, worked on the S&D at Shapwick as a clerk where she met my father, Arthur Badman, who was a signalman on the S&D. He started work as a porter at Burnham-on-Sea in the 1920s, becoming a signalman at Evercreech Junction in 1936, then a relief signalman in 1942. He unfortunately passed away on 27th March 1956, his previous day's work being at Edington Burtle station. My father introduced me to many characters on the S&D. One of these was Guy Parsons who was a porter at Ashcott and lived in the station house. They had a common interest in breeding budgerigars. Guy had utilized the redundant wooden ladies toilet to house his generator which supplied him with light and power for his television. He was very fond of fishing and would sit on the edge of the rhine which was just outside his back door fishing for eels. He told me he would be fishing late at night and his wife would shout out from the bedroom window: "Isn't it about time you came to bed?"

Porter Arthur Badman at Burnham-on-Sea station in the 1920s. (J.Badman collection)

When I was a schoolboy I used to travel to Cole from Evercreech New to Sexey's school. One day I was on the school train and we had just arrived at Evercreech Junction when there was a big commotion. A prisoner was being escorted on the train to Shepton Mallet prison and had made a run for it off the train. Unfortunately for him he was caught. At the time there was a railway detective stationed at Evercreech and he was standing on the platform. A swift rugby tackle brought him down and he was taken into the waiting room whilst other arrangements were made to get him to the prison.

One of the busiest times on the branch was when Glastonbury Tor fair was on. It was always nice to go with my father to this event as he couldn't always get time off from work.

When I left school I started work, like my forefathers, on the S&D. I started on 16th August 1950 at West

Pennard station as a clerk, where the likeable Reg Jeans was the stationmaster. One of the porters there that I remember was Tom (Sailor) Leonard. Most of West Pennard's traffic was cider from the local makers, which reminds me of one of my uncles, Charlie Ham, who was an S&D lorry driver at Glastonbury station. His mate told me of a time in the late 1940s when they went into the British Legion club at Street for some lunchtime refreshment. The barman said to everybody in the bar: "I'll bet you 10/– there is nobody here who could drink a quart of cider straight down in one go." There was no answer, so the barman looked at Charlie and said: "Could you do it?" Charlie replied: "I don't know, I've never tried it; draw one up and we will see." The barman gave Charlie the quart of cider, he picked it up and drank it in one go. He wiped his mouth and said: "O.K. the bet's on, draw me a quart of cider then." That went down the same way in one go. As Charlie said to his mate: "We must come in here more often, two quarts of cider free of charge and a ten bob note."

I spent only a short time at West Pennard as they transferred most of the goods traffic to Glastonbury. I went to Castle Cary for a short time and then left to do my National Service. I rejoined the S&D as a clerk at Evercreech Junction in 1954. Part of my job was making up the pay bills for all the 52 railway staff who worked at the station, including the crossing keepers at Bruton Road, Cockmill and Lamyatt. When you think about it that was a lot of people working at one station. We had eleven shunters for all the traffic that came into the yard. It was an extremely busy time. When the junior porter was not available at Evercreech New I used to go out on the horse and cart with driver George Dyke delivering goods to all the local villages, including Spears sausages made in Bath which were destined for the Post Office and Stores at Ditcheat. There was a very small stable near the station where I used to brush down Prince the delivery horse; he had a lovely temperament.

Sometimes when I was in the office one of the crossing keepers would phone me up on the land line to put a bet on. I would phone it through to the bookmaker at Bruton for him. One day the stationmaster Jack Pike caught me and gave me a telling off as this was not railway work.

When the auditor, Mr Brown, visited us, wearing his old brown suit and speaking with a strong Cockney accent, he was viewed with some concern and considered a bit of a tyrant. We always made sure everything was in order for his visits.

I spent just over a year at Evercreech Junction which I really enjoyed. Unfortunately I was the lowest paid, except for the junior porter, out of the 52 employees. I moved on to Clarks the shoemakers of Street until I eventually retired. The S&D was my family's life and I am glad I was part of it.

1955

John Taylor – Signal & Telegraph Department

I started work on the railway on 31st January 1955 at the Frome signal and telegraph depot (Western region). In October of that year I was appointed assistant lineman on the Frome No 2 section.

In the first week of November 1963 I was relieving the Westbury technician (the lineman grade was changed to technician in the late 50s). Returning to Frome on the late afternoon train on the Friday I was met by our sub-inspector, John Batten, who asked: "Would I mind going over to the Bath S&D section to replace Fred Mitchell who had retired that day [Friday 8th November]?" It would probably only be for a few weeks as the closure of the S&D was still pending. Some of my workmates in the Frome depot warned me that I would get a hostile reception as the men of the S&D hated and detested the Western. This proved to be completely untrue. I was made most welcome and can honestly say that I never had a serious disagreement the whole time I was on the S&D. Of course the line did not close in a few weeks and I was there till the end, two years and five months later.

My assistant was Fred Nicholls, a telegraph wireman from the Shepton Mallet depot. Fred had joined the S&D in the early 1930s and at some time in the 1920s had worked on the Manchester Ship Canal Railway. He was also a part-time sexton at Shepton Parish church. Fred's grandfather, William Nicholls, also worked on the S&D. He was killed with three other men in a rockfall at Winsor Hill on 18th August 1873. Fred was a loyal mate, a keen railwayman and a sincere christian.

My job consisted of maintaining signalbox equipment, block bells, block instruments, signal and lamp repeaters and telephone relays. Outside the box you had the points, signals, ground frames, gates (at Radstock), signal wires, point rodding, overhead line wires and the single-line apparatus at Bath Junction. Working up and down the line there were many S&D fellows like Jock Sommerville (Wellow), Frank Trott (Shepton Mallet), Phil Crouchen and Les Willsher (Radstock), and Ernie Cross (Moorewood), which reminds me of a story.

One morning in 1964 Ernie was in his signalbox at Moorewood sidings when he noticed two men inspecting the disused sidings next to the signalbox. After a time the men entered the box and introduced themselves as the quarry manager and an official from the BR estate office in Bristol. They discussed the removal of the sidings, each man trying to give them to the other. Eventually Ernie said: "As neither of you appear to want to remove them perhaps I could do it for you." With a look of relief on their faces both men agreed that he could remove them providing he cleared the site of all metal and timbers. Later that day Ernie saw the permanent way gang and found out that they didn't have any work on the following Sunday. He told them that he had obtained the job of clearing the sidings and would pay them their usual rate to dismantle the sidings and stack the rails and timbers, to which they agreed. Returning home after his shift, Ernie phoned a scrap merchant and agreed a price. The job was duly carried out, the permanent way gang had an extra day's pay and Ernie made a nice profit for the cost of a phone call.

I recall another story about a signalman on the S&D, who had a lovely garden butting on to one of the stations. He was renowned for having a very short fuse and would blow his top at the thought of any injustice to himself. Visiting the signalbox sometime in 1965 he asked me what was going to happen to a certain box now that it was closed. I told him that it could be bought for £3 provided the purchaser cleared the site. If nobody bought it then it would remain until the line closed completely. The signalman snorted at this and said he would not give £3 for it and anyway he didn't want the box. Now the local permanent way gang, on hearing of this and knowing the signalman's volatile temper, put the story about that their ganger was going to buy the box and make use of the timber upper section. The stone work of the bottom half he would roll down the bank towards the signalman's well-kept garden. On my next visit to this box, the signalman was in a vile mood and demanded to know if anyone had bought the box. I told him nobody had, so he asked me to arrange with the signal and telegraph office for him to buy it for £3. He duly acquired the box. I assume that he used the timber for firewood and I have no idea what he did with the stonework. He certainly bought himself a load of hard work and saved BR hundreds of pounds for not having to demolish the box. But he had saved his garden and that was all he was concerned about.

1955

Peter Pike – Fitter

Templecombe was a railway village where most of the inhabitants worked on the Somerset & Dorset or had relations and friends who did. I became an

A happy group at Evercreech Junction. From left to right, Albert Taylor, Percy Hamblin, Annie Chave (Peter Pike's grandmother), David Kerle and Gwen Pike (Peter's mother). (V.Freak)

apprentice fitter there on 5th April 1955. Other colleagues who worked there at that time were shedmaster Jack Vosper, fitters Frank Iley, Ken Arnott and Bert Hughes, boilersmith Joe Dyer, and clerk Jim Fry. Fitter's mates were Bert Rolls, Arthur Elliot and Bernard Curtis. It was a very busy time looking after the motive power at Templecombe and I worked on most engines like the 7F, 4F, 3F, Black 5 and many others. We had to carry out maintenance repairs and examinations of locos including gland packing, brake blocking, valve and piston removal and re-ringing, which would all be carried out in the running shed.

My first job when I started was working with fitter Bert Hughes and his mate Bernard Curtis. I was using a 14lb sledge hammer to part the piston from the cross head on a class 3F No 43436. I always remember that first day as I went home with a handful of blisters.

Changing brake blocks on SR class G6, No 30274, was not a job we looked forward to as we had to lower the brake hanger and change the blocks, then lift the hanger block back up using a pair of sack trucks as a lever. Then we had to try and line up the hanger and the bracket and replace the hanger pin. This job was a lot more difficult than a straightforward brake block change on our LMS-built engines.

Peter Pike busy with the controls of Ivatt tank No 41304 in March 1963. (P.Pike collection)

I spent a year at Templecombe and then moved on to Bath Green Park to gain more experience. They were a good bunch there. Harold Morris was the shedmaster and he was a very nice chap. Fitters that I recall were Tom Davis, Ray Metcalf and Howard Hiscox, with boilersmith Keith Davey and other apprentices like myself including Eddie Swannack and Brian Davies. I qualified as a fitter in 1960 and moved back to Templecombe where I stayed until 1964.

One of the most hazardous times that I recall was in the winter of 1962/3. Snow like I have never seen before engulfed the whole of the S&D; it was treacherous. Not only did we have to try and keep up with repair work on the engines but we also had to try and keep the injectors on the engines from freezing which was almost an impossible task. We lit cotton waste soaked in paraffin and put it on a shovel, then held it under the injectors and water pipes; this was all one could do. It was a very cold and boring job but it had to be done to make sure the locomotive engines could keep going. One night there was a terrible blizzard. There was only one permanent way man who could get to work because of the weather and he was trying to keep the points clear at No 2 and No 3 Junction but he was fighting a losing battle against the weather. Frank Ray and myself had an idea. We wrapped ourselves up as warm as possible, had a large mug of tea in the messroom, then commandeered a crew and an engine from the shed. We took with us the tube blower's steam lance, sat with our legs dangling over the buffer beam of the engine and started blasting the snow away from the points. It worked a treat and we kept this up on and off for quite a few hours to allow the traffic through. We looked like snowmen perched on the buffers. Again due to the bad weather the wages were unable to get through. I had just arrived for night duty when Harry Jeans, the shedmaster, came into the fitter's shop and explained that the wages were coming via Waterloo and would I come to the station with him to collect them. That night the staff wages made up of hundreds of pounds were hidden in a sack bag under the bench in the fitting shop ready for the morning. The Templecombe lads were a trustworthy bunch and everything was in order for the next day.

Frank Ray holds the lamp on 2P, No 40537, at Templecombe. (P.Pike collection)

I remember being called out one early dark morning at Templecombe to change a gauge glass on a 9F which was working the down mail (2.40am off Bath). As there was a high shoulder of ballast at Templecombe Lower I asked the No 2 signalman to call out to the driver as the train passed to ask him to stop at the platform as I could not manage the climb into the cab. With the high shoulder of ballast this manoeuvre took a few minutes longer. The driver kindly stopped at the platform for me and I duly changed the broken glass. A few days later the shedmaster Harry Jeans had a letter of complaint from the Royal Mail demanding I had a reprimand for delaying Her Majesty's mail train by five minutes. Harry's remarks about the Royal Mail were unprintable. He told me not to worry, and to forget about it and I heard no more.

How nice it would be to turn the clock back to those days, where friendship and comradeship were second to none. My regular mate, Frank Ray, was a special workmate and friend who never complained when he had to help me into a loco cab and also when carrying out motion work. This help was needed because of partial paralysis due to polio. Frank and I remained firm friends up to the time of his sad death. He was a real mate whom I miss very much. His memory will always stay with me as does the Somerset and Dorset Railway.

1956

Terry Fry – Fireman

I spent 10 years on the Somerset and Dorset Railway as a fireman at Highbridge and as a driver on the branch at Bridgwater. Some of the senior drivers who helped me a lot at Highbridge were Harry Pearce, Charlie King, Bill Peck, Bill May and Ronald Andrews.

The most memorable trip that I recall happened in the winter of 1962/3. I was a fireman at the time and my driver was the well-known Ronald (Chummy) Andrews. Chummy started on the S&D in 1914 giving 50 years service to the railway he loved. He spent all his working life on the branch except for a short period at Bath. He was a true S&D railwayman and an excellent engineman. I recall we often brought back bags of peat on the footplate from Ashcott for his friends in Highbridge.

Chummy and myself were taking the last passenger train of the day, the 7.10pm from Highbridge to Evercreech Junction. Driver Bill May had brought the previous train in from Evercreech; he came over to us and said it was the worst conditions he had seen since he had been on the S&D which in 1963 had been 43 years service. The snow was so deep he had trouble getting through and strongly warned us that we were going into blizzard conditions the like we had never seen before. Our engine was a class 2MT, No 41296, and we had two carriages on. The passengers were now on board and we set off. It was everything Bill had said and as we were going through Bason Bridge and Edington the weather was getting worse by the minute. Snow was everywhere, it was a white wilderness, very eerie with a creepy silence. We got to Glastonbury and fortunately the last passengers got out. Chummy was working miracles with the regulator and I was firing the best I could in the circumstances. The wind was biting and the snow was gushing in all over the footplate; we looked like two abominable snowmen. I must say that our old engine was working very well in these snowy conditions. Our guard, Jack Alford, was in the van. Hopefully he had the steam heat radiators on as if not, in these conditions, he would have been frozen solid. We arrived at Pylle Halt; the station was locked up and as we were attempting to leave Pylle a large snowdrift stopped our movement under the A37 roadbridge. We couldn't go backwards or forwards. Chummy tried everything but with no joy. It was now getting serious. The snow was getting worse and we were going nowhere. After a quick discussion with Chummy and Jack, Chummy decided that he

From left to right, Maurice Cook, Terry Fry, Mike Lewis and George Wheadon stand in front of a pair of Colletts, Nos 3216 and 3206, at Highbridge motive power depot. (M.Cook collection)

had to get to Evercreech Junction signalbox to get help in pulling us out. He made his way out of the station with the tablet in his hand which would allow him access on the single line, hopefully back to Pylle. As he disappeared out of sight we both thought that this was a brave act in trying to get help. All telephone communications were down, we couldn't put detonators down onto the track as the snow was too thick, but we made sure a red light was on the front of our engine to warn any incoming traffic. A couple of hours went by. Where was Chummy, was he all right, had he got through? I thought I could hear a whistle and looked out of the cab but I couldn't see anything, just a continual white haze. Then suddenly I heard a long whistle and the most welcoming sight I have ever seen, a class 3F driven by a Radstock crew with a snow plough on the front and Chummy acting as a pilot in the cab. The 3F set to work, with Chummy and I clearing the snow from under the engine's wheels with shovels. After about an hour we slowly moved off following the 3F into Evercreech Junction which was about two miles away. We were all very pleased to arrive safely at Evercreech and to have a hot cup of tea and warm in the porters' cabin at the end of the platform.

After leaving us, Chummy had knocked on various station cottages and found somebody with a car who was willing to make the hazardous journey to Evercreech. Fortunately one railwayman volunteered and as Chummy said to me later: "How we got to Evercreech in the car I shall never know." It was a trip never to be forgotten and little did we know that the winter of 1962/63 was one of the worst in living memory.

1956

Tom Cox – Boilerwasher

I joined the railway in January 1956 at Bath Green Park locomotive shed as a coalman, my earnings were £4 10s per week. The job consisted of shovelling coal from 15-ton trucks into 10-cwt steel four-wheel tubs and placing them against the coal stage wall ready to tip the coal into the engine's tender. We moved about 20 to 30 tons of coal per eight-hour shift, and it was hard work. Other coalmen there at this time were Jimmy Cockerell and George Heniman.

From coaling I moved on to boilerwashing which involved taking plugs out of engine boilers and extracting mudhole covers from under the side of the engine. We then washed scale out of the engine boiler with a high pressure water hose until the inside of the boiler was clean. We also had to examine the inside of the boiler with a light taped onto a long piece of stiff wire. A fellow boilerwasher at the time was Reg Greenman. There was an inspector who travelled around the area inspecting boilers that were having a big examination. If it was a normal wash out, our own boilersmith, Ivor Musty, examined the boiler. After he had examined the boiler and it was all certified in order he would shout out: "Box her up", and I would have to replace the plugs, mudhole covers and inspection covers on top of the engine. After all that was carried out we would fill the boiler back up with water, making sure that there were no leaky joints. The engine would then be ready for the steamraiser to light up.

The shedmaster at Bath was Mr Harold Morris. He was one of the old brigade, a tall, slim man who always wore a smart suit, a trilby hat and had a gold watch chain. He used to come around and see everybody including us at the coal stage where the dust was flying everywhere. We were black as soot, sweat pouring off us, but he always made a point of coming to see us. He would say "all right, Tom?" and offer you a cigarette from his gold cigarette case. He would have a smoke with you and thank you for the work you were doing and wish you a good day.

We were expected to cover for the steamraisers when they went on holiday or went sick. Your first job was to make sure the engine boiler was filled up to about the quarter mark on the water gauge on the footplate. You would open the firehole doors and place a half circle of coal or briquettes on the grate below the door. You would then drop in about four fire-lighters, put some more coal on top of them and add some paraffin waste, light it and drop it into the half circle of coal. Then you would place a small amount of coal on top and leave it to burn for a while. You had to go back later after the coal fire had burnt up, push it forward a bit and put some more coal on the fire and open the dampers to help the fire burn. After a time, when the steam pressure was raised, you used the injectors to fill the boiler and tried to keep about 80 lbs of steam for the fireman who came aboard the engine.

Sometimes you had as many as 18 engines to look after around the shed at the same time, checking each of them every so often to ensure that everything was all right. You paid more attention to the first engines off shed, making sure they were not blowing off steam too much. You had all different types of engines like class 2Ps, Standard 5s, 4Fs, 7Fs and 9Fs. I also carried out steam-raising at Radstock shed where the shunting and banking engines were stabled. It was a lonely and frightening experience as you were on your own in the shed from about 10.00pm till the first shunters' crew came on duty about 2.30am. I remember I used to put a form up against the shed door. There were squeaks and groans coming from everywhere including the engines as they warmed up.

I was in Bath shed when we had a runaway. It was in the summer working time when the outlying shunters' crew used to come in from Radstock and Midsomer Norton to help out. On this particular day a Greenback (West

Country class) was being coaled up and went up to the bank to reverse back into the shed for maintenance. But in reversing it came charging down the bank with sirens wailing (an American type of hooter). The engine went through the shed buffer into the chargeman's wooden hut, through the quarterway and ended up in the driving crews' messroom. It caused a hell of a mess, there was mayhem and panic everywhere, but luckily nobody was hurt. The cause of the problem was that one of the crew did not apply the brake properly. I gather he was not used to big engines, only the small Jinty tanks.

Another memory comes to mind when I was up in the coal stage, tipping coal into what I thought was the engine's tender only to find I had tipped it all into the cab and the driver was standing in the middle of it. Luckily it was only small northern coal so the driver was not hurt but he certainly wasn't amused.

The winter of 1963 was one of the worst winters that I can remember in my lifetime. I was a boilerwasher at the time and I remember having to light the coal-fired brazier to keep the water pipes from freezing at our engine shed, which was wooden and in a very dilapidated condition. The snow used to blow in all over the place and working there was very uncomfortable and draughty. I remember someone lit a fire in the shed and part of the wooden wall burnt down; we all had a laugh about that.

We also had to help in the coal stage. The coal was frozen in the trucks and had to be hacked out with a pick-axe. Snow, coal and ice all went into the engine tender making life very difficult. At that time I did not have a car and I remember pushing my bicycle to work in two to three feet of snow. During that time one of our trains got stuck in a snowdrift at Masbury on the Mendips. The engine crew didn't get back home for nearly 24 hours, having had to trudge through deep snow to get help. They sent out a relief breakdown gang to dig the train out and I believe that it got stuck as well.

I helped prepare one of the last trains to go down on the S&D, by painting the smokebox and making sure the engine was generally tidy. It was a very sad day. I spent 35 years on British Rail, including 10 years on the S&D, retiring on 24th October 1991. I can still remember some of my S&D colleagues at Bath, running foreman Fred Holmes, Leslie Thorne and Bert Clarke, both fitter's mates, and Jim Jefferies, chargeman cleaner.

1957

Gerry White – Porter

Evercreech New station was a great place to work. I started there in 1957, and spent seven years at the station. I began as a porter carrying out the issuing and collecting of tickets, weighing parcels and looking after the passengers.

It was a full-time working station and besides your normal duties you worked in the goods yard. The up siding was mainly used by the coal merchants, Brown's and Alan Feaver & Company. The down siding was used for loading and unloading grain driers from Gascoigne's, milk powder tins that came from National Dried Milk to be filled at Prideaux's.

Evercreech New station. BR Standard class 4, No 75023, pilots a modified West Country, possibly No 34028, Eddystone, *with a northbound train. (E.Rimmer)*

One day I was helping out the shunter, we were shunting some coal wagons. I had my brake stick stuck in the brake mechanism on one of these wagons when suddenly it broke away with me hanging onto the brake stick trying to bring it to a standstill. It ran towards Evercreech Junction wrong line and as it passed the signalbox I spotted Reg Jeans the stationmaster. I shouted out to him: "I can't stop it, I can't stop it." It must have looked funny, me running and hanging on for dear life trying to stop this runaway coal truck. I eventually stopped it just before the crossovers; I was completely shattered. Reg Jeans was a superb artist and next day he brought in a humorous cartoon of myself hanging on desperately to the runaway wagon. Reg also enjoyed model railways. In his loft he had a full working model set out in true S&D fashion, with trains always running to time.

On one occasion Charlie Hartnell, the goods checker, and myself were loading a large grain drier from a lorry onto a Conflat D truck in the down siding. We had got it off the lorry and were manoeuvering it onto the truck when it slipped and part of it was now hanging over the main line. We then heard the thump of the signal arm and realized a train had left Shepton Mallet and was going over Prestleigh Viaduct. We frantically heaved and shoved this grain drier away from the line. We could hear the bark of the engine getting nearer and nearer. Charlie and myself gave it one more heave with the pinch bar and finally got it on the Conflat truck with only a minute to spare before the engine would have made contact with it.

I remember one amusing story about my mate Charlie Hartnell. He and his wife were going on holiday, and he had brought their cases down to the station. While he wasn't looking, we put a load of confetti in them, then waved them goodbye. On their return Mrs Hartnell came up to us and said: "What the bloody hell do you think we wanted, another honeymoon?" We all had a jolly good laugh, but poor old Charlie was in the doghouse for weeks after.

Even though we were a small station we had our own Thornycroft lorry, registration No JXA 312, complete with three articulated trailers, two flat beds and one box van. After several years I took over the driving job from Clive Withers. We used to send cream by passenger train. Prideaux's would phone to say there was another batch to collect and more than once the train was held up if we were running a bit late.

You could set your clock at 9.00pm when the Perisher left Evercreech Junction dead on time; you could hear her whistle as she left. In the summer months the holiday specials returning to the Midlands had to stop at Evercreech New. If it was a Southern engine crew and they needed a banker you could hear them saying to the signalman: "Here comes that dirty banking engine." They thought their Southern engines were much cleaner than ours on the S&D.

We had a lengthman's hut at the New; I often went in there to enjoy a hot cup of tea. Dennis Poore was the driver of the engineer's trolley that was used by the permanent way gang.

The S&D staff were a good bunch of fellows to work with, people like father and son Don and Bill Webb, Derek 'Tanker' Jones, Ern Harrup, Terry Bond, Joe Gould, Ted Simms and Ted Lambert. The S&D was a wonderful railway. When Prestleigh Viaduct was blown up a couple of years back I kept one of the stones as a permanent reminder of the S&D.

1960

David Hughes – Porter

My S&D days started at Sturminster Newton in 1960 as a goods porter. My duties consisted of loading and unloading goods wagons, parcels, cattle feeds, preparing cattle pens for the local market and washing them down at the end of the day. It was a busy life then in that farming community. You had to assist with the shunting and generally keep the yard and goods office tidy. I moved to Stalbridge as a platform porter in 1962, where my job entailed meeting and attending all passenger trains, collecting tickets, checking all carriage doors and giving the guard the signal to pull away. Part of the job was to clean and fill the signal lamps with oil at one end of the station section one day and the next day do the same at the other end of the section. In the summer months, while out lamping the distant signal at Stalbridge, I often wandered into a field and picked a bag of mushrooms. In the springtime I would also pick a few wild flowers from the bank. I used to enjoy a cup of tea with the gangers in their hut. Their tea was something not to be missed, it was black and you could almost stand your spoon in it. I enjoyed their company; the whole line was friendly, it was a way of life on the S&D.

One memory I have which emphasises this was when I was out on lamping duties in the summer months. A goods or passenger train would be passing and the footplate crew would signal with a wave and a whistle to a local farmer and his workers, who would be haymaking in a nearby field. In turn the farmer who was sitting on his tractor would raise his cap and the farm workers would wave back. If it was their break time a jar of scrumpy was raised as they sat on bales of hay.

Another recollection that comes to mind, was when visiting a resident crossing keeper who never had running water in his cottage. The goods trains would stop and the driver and fireman would take churns of water off the side of the engine and take them into the crossing keeper's house. This was greeted with a hot cup of tea, and if the weather was really hot they would have a glass or two of ice cold orange squash. The keeper would then take a drink to the guard at the rear of the train. No one was ever forgotten, and that was what was so good about the old line.

Part of my duties was to look after the flower beds at the station. One summer's day I was working away planting seedlings into the borders when the resident stationmaster Sidney Cox came up to me. He complimented me on my work in the garden and then said: "There is one thing missing." I looked up and said: "What's that, Mr Cox?" He said: "Don't forget to whitewash the stones around the borders." It was detail like this that made the flower garden such a spectacular sight in the spring and summer months.

Being young and carefree I once upset the local policeman. It was around November 5th, bonfire night. Charlie Meachem, the village bobby, would come up to the signalbox and have a cup of tea and a chat with the signalman. After about 30 minutes he would make his way onto his beat stopping off at the toilet as he went. Well I had these "little demon" and "thunderflash" fireworks. As Charlie went to the toilet I lit a "little demon" and threw it over the toilet wall; seconds later there was a terrific flash, a shout and Charlie came running out in some disarray. He saw me and chased me down the platform. I kept my head down for the next few days when Charlie came for his cup of tea. He was a good sort and later saw the funny side of it.

Stalbridge was an idyllic spot in the summer, but the winter of 1962/63 was a different matter. It was quite an unbelievable scene, everywhere you looked there were snowdrifts. There was no movement on the roads or anywhere else. As railwaymen we made a determined effort to keep our village station open. I had to refill the distant lamps, not a pleasant job bearing in mind the snow was three feet deep with bitter easterly winds, but I managed it. I recall many times tramping back in blizzards to Stalbridge station, my whole body absolutely frozen. It was heaven when a passing goods train came your way; they would always stop and pick you up, give you a cup of tea and drop you off at the station. You headed straight for the cosy gangers' hut which was situated in the sidings next to Stalbridge station. The stove would be burning bright and my workmates and me would hover over the fire warming ourselves with a hot steaming cup of tea. Mr Cox and the district inspector often came into the hut in this period and would have a cup of tea with us. When leaving to visit other stations along the line I will always remember the district inspector saying: "Well done lads, keep up the good work." He thanked us for looking after them, and said: "If you run short of coal for the hut just get the crew to drop off a few lumps of coal as they pass by."

In the latter part of 1963 I moved to Henstridge station as a leading porter which meant you did everything from issuing tickets, attending to the oil lamps, operating the ground frame to working the single-line token for going in and out of the small siding. I stayed until the closure of the S&D. People I worked with and knew were fireman Roy Curtis, driver Rodney Scovell, lorry driver Ted Drew, guard Reg Brewer, signalmen Bob Downes and John Cluett.

Henstridge station staff standing on the platform in 1938. From left to right, Joe Coward, stationmaster Alan Whitehead and Peter Jackson. (E.Coward collection)

Countless words have been said by so many about their love of the Somerset and Dorset Railway. I can only endorse the same feelings. It was a marvellous railway to work on with a real sense of comradeship that I am so glad to have experienced, one big happy family.

1962

David Walker – Passed Cleaner

When I was younger I lived with my mother, two brothers, and one sister at Cheriton crossing, between Wincanton and Templecombe. It was a two up, two down crossing house with an outside toilet and very crowded for a family of five.

In 1962 I started work at Templecombe as a cleaner, later becoming a passed cleaner. Depending on who the driver was I used to shovel coal off the tender as we went by our crossing house; I always got a wave from my mother. During our stay there, trains ran through the gates twice. I cannot recall what the circumstances were but we always teased her about it. One caller to the crossing was the lampman, Jock Nicol, who worked from Wincanton. He used to start the day off from the porters' cabin (on the down platform) and cook his egg and bacon on the little black stove. I remember his boots were always highly polished, he wore a bib and brace, and his trouser bottoms were kept up by cycle clips. He cleaned all the signal lamps and refilled them at various locations. Jock was very meticulous in carrying out his work in all types of weather and was a happy cheerful fellow who epitomized the S&D railwayman.

Cheriton crossing showing the usual S&D keeper's cottage with all the standard trappings including the very large television aerial. (D.Milton)

When I started cleaning I can recall to this day shovelling out hot coals from fireboxes on various engines which were brought back to the depot, getting underneath the engines in the pit raking out the ashpans, the dust clogging up your nose and mouth, and the smell of the steam given off when you dampened down the ashes. I also helped coal up the locomotives and remember very well Walter Webb operating the crane and bucket; he was always a very friendly and cheerful person. As a cleaner, part of your job was to polish all the brass work inside the cabs. I remember having spent two whole days cleaning the outside of a BR class 5 loco, including the tender, with a mixture of paraffin and oil which made the paintwork shine; I also repainted the buffer beams. I felt really proud watching this engine taking the train to Bath, it looked brand new.

The first time I went inside a firebox I was very scared, I had this fear of the firebox doors closing behind me and being suffocated from the sulphur fumes. I would also help the boiler men replace the grates or the brick arches and clean the tubes that had become blocked, with tube brushes. At 16 years of age I went on a course to Bath to qualify as a passed cleaner which enabled me to carry out firing duties. I couldn't wait to pass the exams and can still recall today Rule 55, the longest rule in the rule book.

My first firing duties were on the shunting engines which worked in Templecombe yard. One of the drivers, Fritz Lawrence, really had me going. The cab had to be spotless, brasses kept highly polished, the floor washed and coal damped down so there was no dust. He told me off if I was firing when I should be looking out for signals or giving instructions to him too late. But it

91

did make me feel important and I couldn't wait to work on a proper firing turn as I called it. The first of these was on the Templecombe to Highbridge line. It was on the Highbridge branch line that I had my most memorable experience. My driver was the legendary Ronald (Chummy) Andrews and we were on a GWR Collett engine, No 3206. Soon after leaving Evercreech Mr Andrews asked me what I would do if he was to collapse or have a heart attack. I replied: "I'd take control of the engine till the next station." He then said: "Well I'm now unconscious, you take the controls." For a lad of 16 to drive a steam train was fantastic, a dream come true. He let me drive it from Pylle to Bason Bridge, stopping at each station.

Another memorable experience was the day when I was fireman to Tom Kesteven. This was my first trip over the Mendips to Bath on a fast passenger train from Templecombe; the engine was a BR Standard 4, No 75073. I now felt I was a fireman at last, but found it very hard work; going into the long tunnel at Combe Down for the first time was very frightening. On one occasion when we had a blowback in the tunnel I nearly jumped off the engine as the cab filled up with flames and sparks; thank goodness for a wet cloth to cover your face to stop the smoke getting into your eyes and lungs. Tom was a church organist and while going over the Mendips he would be singing out loud to the rhythm of the locomotive. That meant everything was going well. I was paired with Tom on quite a few occasions working to Bath and Bournemouth.

One morning at about 4.00am I heard a noise outside our crossing house, then tapping on the window. I was in big trouble: I had overslept. They sent out

BR Standard class 4, No 75073, takes water at Evercreech Junction with a southbound train in 1957. Notice the BR emblem on the tender, the fire devil under the water column and the leading ex-LMS brake with the guard's look-out at the very front. (R.E.Toop)

a light engine to pick me up from the crossing, getting special permission to go back wrong line to Templecombe shed. There are not many people who can say they got a lift to work on a steam engine from their front door.

Another time, again at night, we were woken up by the sound of something going up and down the line. We knew there were no trains at 1 o'clock in the morning. Going to investigate we could see a single goods wagon on the up line rolling backwards and forwards, so mum phoned the signalman at Templecombe No 2 box. Initially he thought my mum was having him on. After investigation it was found to be a wagon that had rolled out of Templecombe Upper yard, down past No 2 box, passing Horsington crossing before it got to us at Cheriton. The wagon was retrieved by an engine from Evercreech.

One day at Templecombe shed I had a lucky escape whilst coupling up some wagons in the sidings. I heard a loud hissing sound so I came out from between the engine and wagon to see what it was. A light engine was coming towards the yard; its steam brakes had failed and it was going very fast. The points were set for the siding where I was coupling up and it was coming towards me and my engine. I saw the driver and fireman leap from the engine just yards away from impact. The damage to the engines was quite considerable.

I spent four years on the S&D. I was very lucky to have had the chance to fire various engines, Bulleid Pacifics, 9Fs and of course the good old 7Fs. I fired to many drivers, Ray Stokes, Percy Hobbs, Walt Jeans, Gerald Trowbridge, Fred Fisher and Les Warren. Living on the S&D and working on it was an exciting time for a 16-year old. I'm very glad that I worked in the steam era and proud to have served on the Somerset and Dorset railway.

The mock funeral at Evercreech Junction to commemorate the closure of the S&D on 5th March 1966. The pallbearers are Vic Freak (back left), the unseen Alec Stowe, Charlie Vaughan (front left) and Eddie Riggs. The undertaker is Les Marsh. (V.Freak collection)

INDEX (numbers in **bold** indicate a chapter, numbers in *italic* indicate a photograph)

Jack Alford	83-84	
Bill Amos	37	
Ronald 'Chummy' Andrews		
	16, 51, 83-4, 92	
Ken Arnott	81	
Bert Ash	7	
Reg Ashford	16	
Dennis Ashill	64	
Gilbert Ashill	64, *64*	
Ned Ashman	38	
Tom Ashman	30	
Ken Atkins	30, 70	
Charlie Attwood	15	
George Austin	61	
Arthur Badman	77, *77*	
Florence Badman	77	
John Badman	**76-78**	
Bill Bailey	63-64	
Sam Bailey	70	
Arthur Baker	52	
Bert Baker	43	
Charlie Baker	6	
Ernest Baker	74	
Mike Baker	43	
Phyllis Baker	52	
Sally Baker	52	
Keith Barrett	43	
Ralph Barry	44	
Tom Bass	48	
Ray Batt	15	
John Batten	79	
Cyril Beale	32	
Donald Beale	29, 64	
Ron Bean	28	
Fred Beard	7, 16	
Reg Beasley	17-18, 20	
Bill Beeho	6, 17-18	
Margaret Beeho	17	
Mervyn Belbin	42	
Joyce Bell (née Pearce)	**51-53**	
Hugh Berryman	76, *76*	
Harry Biffin	48	
Dickie Bird	28	
Percy Bishop	70	
Alec Bolwell	39, 64	
Terry Bond	88	
Dave Boston	**57-61**	
Fred Box	28, 29, 30	
Freda Box	**28-30**	
Jim Brabner	44	

Bill Brady	44-45	
Frank Braund	47	
Bert Brewer	64	
Reg Brewer	28, 90	
Colin Brine	2	
Charlie Brown	35	
Harry Brown	12, 48	
Mr Brown, Auditor	78	
Jocky Bullock	32	
Ian Bunnett	9	
Clive Burden	65-66, *66*	
Percy Burt	20	
Reg Burt	20	
Vic Burt	**20-22**	
Jim Cantello	61	
George Carey	73-74	
Herbie Carter	14	
Percy Carter	77	
Sid Cater	63	
Pip Chant	54	
Annie Chave	*80*	
Harry Clark	7	
Bert Clarke	*60*, 86	
Dennis Clem	8, 36	
Arthur Clist	64	
John Cluett	90	
Jimmy Cockerell	85	
Bert Colbourn	50	
Wilf Coleman	74	
Bill Conibeer	13	
Ern Cook	45	
Jack Cook	63	
Maurice Cook	**12-13**, *13*, 44, *84*	
Norman Cook	7, **44-48**	
Ted Cook	70	
Charlie Cooksley	43	
Bill Coomer	49	
Bill Cornell	7	
Herbie Cornish	49	
George Coward	43	
Joe Coward	*90*	
Bill Cox	43	
Sidney Cox	89	
Tom Cox	**84-86**	
Ernie Cross	61, 79	
Phil Crouchen	79	
Bernard Curtis	81	
Evelyn Curtis	38	
Harry Curtis	16	
Roy Curtis	90	

Les Cuss	65-66	
Reg Darke	**37-43**, *37*	
Keith Davey	81	
Brian Davies	81	
Trevor Davies	10-11	
Charlie Davis	11	
Fred Davis	7	
Mr Davis, Stationmaster	5	
Tom Davis	81	
Cliff Day	43, *67*	
Arthur Derrick	32	
George Dewfall	48	
Jack Dowell	32, 42	
Charlie Dowling	49	
Bob Downes	90	
Bob Drew	58, 61	
Ted Drew	90	
Hugh Durston	70	
Ben Dyer	63, 64, 65, 75	
Joe Dyer	64, 81	
George Dyke	78	
Joe Easterbrook	*60*	
Reg Eaton	51	
Eric Elford	29, 64	
Arthur Elliot	81	
Ted Elliot	75	
Len England	10	
Fred Epps	**22-25**, *23*	
Pat Evans	67	
Ken Eveleigh	68	
Alec Fear	38-39	
Fred Fisher	93	
Joan Fisher	76	
Susie Fisher	52	
John Flynn	64	
Basil Foote	43	
Charlie Ford	44	
Bert Fortune	57	
Jack Foxhall	15	
Arthur Francis	30	
Vic Freak	2, 30, *43*, 93	
Bert Freakley	64	
Bob Fry	16, 70-72, 74	
Jim Fry	81	
Paul Fry	**70-74**	
Terry Fry	**83-84**, *84*	
Jim Garland	15	

Percy Gedge 63
Frank Germain 49
Fred Gibbons 5
Bert Gibbs 48
Ray Gibbs 44
Bill Goddard 20, 38
Albert Good 43
Jimmy Good 65, *65*
Joe Gould 88
Robin Gould 20
Roy Gould 15
Edgar Gray 22, 25
Ron Gray 29, 63
Bob Green 18
George Green *43*
Reg Greenman 85
Fred Griffin 16, 49
Archie Gunning 11, *11*, 12, 28
Bill Gunning 11, *11*, 12
Tom Gunning 37
Charlie Guy 53
Ernie Guy 48, 52

David Hadfield 10
Les Haines 44
Charlie Ham 78
Edmond Ham 76-77
Renee Ham 52
Percy Hamblin 18, *80*
Charles Hamilton 27
Bert Hansford 45
Horace Hardridge 44
Norman Harrison 49
Ern Harrup 88
Charlie Hartnell 87, 88
Jack Harvey 71, *71*, 72
Art Hatcher 54, 65, *65*, 74-75
Gordon Hatcher 20, **53-54**, *54*
Malcolm Hatherall 15-16
Ernie Hemmings 24
George Heniman 85
Bert Henman 58-59
Wilf Hickman 74
Howard Hiscox 4, 81
Alan Hix 65-66, *66*
Jack Hix 65-66
Ernie Hobbs 32
Percy Hobbs 93
Ralph Holden 32
Fred Holmes 86
John Holt **74-76**, *75*
Jack Hopkins 11
Harry Hovey 25
Bert Hughes 81

David Hughes **88-90**

Frank Iley 81

Peter Jackson *90*
George James 44
Harry Jeans 64, 82
Reg Jeans 72, 73, 74, 78, 87
Walt Jeans 93
Jim Jefferies 86
Henry Jennings 6
Bert Jones 39, 40, 65
David Jones 7
Derek 'Tanker' Jones 88
Frank Jones 16
Stan Jones 49
Steve Jones 7-8
Mr Joseph, Stationmaster 49

Jack Kemp 6
Joe Kemp 30
David Kerle *80*
Tom Kesteven 92
Bernard Kilmister **32-37**
Arthur King **31-32**
Charlie King 45, *52*, 69, 83
Gordon King 36
Jock Kirkbright 16
Charlie Knight 22-23

Mark Lambert **54-55**
Ted Lambert **43-44**, *43*, 88
Alan Larcombe 60-61
Fritz Lawrence 65, 91
Bert Lee 37
Bill Lee 37
Wilf Lee 5
May Leigh 52
Tom Leonard 78
Fred Lester 64
Danny Levi 32
Mike Lewis *84*
Mr H Lewis, Stationmaster 7
Charlie Light 41
Norman Light 20
Jack Loader, clerk 6
Jack Loader, driver 37
Will Locke 64
Mary Lockwood 30
Norman Lockwood 30
Lou Long 65-66, *66*

Jim Machin 62
Larry Maggs 19-20, 35, 51, 53

Les Marsh *93*
David Massey 28
Mick Matthews 48
Bill May 16, 45, 83
Charlie Meachem 89
Harry Meader 48
Jack Meaker 44
Nathaniel Meech 76
George Merchant 64
Alf Metcalf 11
Ray Metcalf 81
Eric Miles **67-70**
Joyce Miles 69
Maurice Miles 20
Roy Miles **55-57**, *57*, 67-68
Fred Mitchell 79
Jim Mogg 5
Wally Moon 16
Ron Moore 59
Harold Morris 81, 85
Colonel Mountstevens 16
Lou Moxey 12
Tom Mundy 43
Ivor Musty 85

Trevor Netley 65
Bill Newman 55
Bill Newton 49
Michael Newton 49
Bill Nicholls 37
Fred Nicholls 79
William Nicholls 79
Jock Nicol 90
David Norman *26*
John Norman 5-6
Den Norris 9, 41, *75*
Ken Norris 32, 59-60

Jack Osborne 76
Christopher Oxford 15

Charlie Packer 48
Frank Packer 28
Frank Padfield 30
Kath Parker *41*
Bill Parrett *26*
Bill Parsons 44
Guy Parsons 77
Percy Parsons 70
Ted Parsons 19
Walt Parsons 44
Ivor Patrick 61
Aubrey Pearce 6
Harry Pearce 16, 45, 51-52, *52*, 74, 83

95

Maurice Pearce 6
Reg Pearce 52
Paul Pearman 9
Bill Peck 45, 83
Steve Penny 20
Albert Perkins 58
Charlie Perkins 58, 61
Ivo Peters 58
Ern Phillips 2
Ern Pike 70
Gwen Pike *80*
Jack Pike 2, 29, 78
Peter Pike **80-83**, *81*
Bill Pitman 43
Osmond Pitt 8, 25, 26, 28
Dick Player 7
Len Pond *62*
Dennis Poore 88
Bill Potter 74
Albert Powis 68
Fred Preater **5-6**
Charlie Preston 68
Bill Prior 43
Ern Pritchard 48
Percy Purnell 14

Sam Randall 37
Bill Rawles 28
Charlie Rawles 14
Charlie Rawlings 6, 7, 16
Frank Ray 81-82, *82*, 83
Eddie Riggs *93*
Theresa Roberts (née Perry)
48-51, *49*
George Robertson 9
Bert Rolls 81
Fred Rooke 11
Norman Rosenburg 32
Mike Ryall 63
Joe Ryan 44
Len Ryan 61

Victor Salway 74
Ernie Sams 38
Bill Sargeant 44
Percy Savage 8, 20
Rodney Scovell 90
Arthur Selman 9-10
Harry Shearn 18
Ron Shearn 35
Bill Silk **63-67**, *66*
Ted Simms 88
George Smart 61
Cliff Smith **61-63**, *62*

Edgar Smith 15, 32
Peter Smith 9, 29
Jock Sommerville 79
Bill Southway 15
John Spencer 61
Frank Staddon **14-20**, *14*, 28, 31
Reg Staddon 32
John Stamp 10-11
Ray Stokes 65, 67, 93
Alec Stowe *43*, 65-66, *93*
Tom Strike 12, 48
Jack Swain 44
Eddie Swannack 81

Albert Taylor *80*
John Taylor **78-80**
Leslie Thorne 86
Bill Thornton 61
Jim Towels 61
Frank Trott 79
Gerald Trowbridge 93
George Tucker **25-28**, *26*, 63
Sam Tucker 15
Fred Turland 5
Arthur Turner 32, 63
Arthur Turvy 33
Frank Tutton 61

Hilda Underwood 52

Charlie Vaughan 54, *93*
Bert Veasey 11
Jack Vosper 81

Christopher Wagner 5
Jack Walbridge *60*
David Walker **90-93**
Johnny Walker 29, 36, 54
Bernard Ware **7-12**
Henry Ware 7
Les Warren 93
Walt Warren 25
Jim Watkins 5
Bill Webb 88
Don Webb 88
Walt Webb 64, 91
Len West 32
George Wheadon 52, *84*
Kit Wheadon 52
Alfred Whitaker 36
Harry Whitaker 36
Gerry White **86-88**
Joe White 5
Sid White 32

Tom White 27
Alan Whitehead *90*
Harold 'Nobby' Whiting *96*
Albert Wilcox 32
Bill Wilds 8
Les Williams 30
Luke Williams 43
Roy Williams *62*
Les Willsher 79
Bill Wiltshire 20
Harry Wiltshire 8
Dick Windsor 36-37
Clive Withers 88
Teddy Woods 49
Roy Woolley 11
Bill Wotton 74

Porter Harold 'Nobby' Whiting on the station platform at Sturminster Newton in the 1930s. (H.Whiting collection)